Mary Elizabeth Earle's life was a tapestry of triumph and tribulation, woven with threads of pain, resilience, and an unwavering spirit. Born in 1947, she faced a childhood marred by an emotionally distant mother and a father whose temperament oscillated between tenderness and explosive outbursts. Enveloped in a cocoon of terror and loneliness, Mary retreated into herself, haunted by nightmares that bore witness to her feeling of being unwanted.

At the tender age of 15, Mary believed she had found her 'Knight in Shining Armour', only to be betrayed by his unsavoury actions, thrusting her into a deeper abyss of suffering that would echo through her life. A violent attack within her marriage plunged her into despair and terror, yet it also unveiled her psychic abilities and the presence of Angels, a revelation that shook her to the core.

Despite the turmoil, an intense longing burned within Mary, fuelling her with a newfound courage to embark on a life-changing journey. This path was fraught with ups and downs, moments of despair and elation, ultimately leading to a broken heart. Yet, like a phoenix rising from the ashes, Mary emerged with a renewed optimism, dedicating her life to helping others heal from their emotional turmoil as a counsellor, trauma specialist, healer, and clairvoyant.

In her book, *The Longing*, Mary shines a light on a shameful period in history, offering solace and understanding to those whose lives were blighted, much like her own. With raw honesty, she shares her personal story of suffering and abuse, a testament to the indomitable human spirit and a beacon of hope for those seeking inspiration amidst the darkest of times.

**Mary Elizabeth Earle**

# THE LONGING

*May your life be paved with happiness*

*Mary Elizabeth Earle*

AUSTIN MACAULEY PUBLISHERS™

LONDON · CAMBRIDGE · NEW YORK · SHARJAH

A CIP catalogue record for this title is available from the British Library.

ISBN 9781035846092 (Paperback)
ISBN 9781035846108 (ePub e-book)

www.austinmacauley.com

First Published 2024
Austin Macauley Publishers Ltd®
1 Canada Square
Canary Wharf
London
E14 5AA

# Acknowledgements

A huge thank you to my family and friends, even strangers I've met along the way, who have encouraged me to write this book. I've been amazed by their love and kindness, which has kept me writing. And to Cafe Copywriter, Kate Philbin, whose guidance and support brought *The Longing* to its final stage. My friend, Marie, deserves a mention for her compassionate reading of my book and the hugs she gave me. Jan, your beautiful art work helped inspire the book cover. How can I not acknowledge the Angelic Realms, to whom I am deeply connected, for their loving presence when I struggled, felt unsure of myself, and was emotionally overwhelmed.

# Table of Contents

Truth is not always easy to voice; we have to be brave. Sometimes the truth we hold onto tightly, eats away at us. Find your courage, speak out, free yourself. Let that hidden part of yourself shine.

# Chapter 1
## *I'm Free*

I slowly closed the lid of my desk, the graffiti and carved grooves the same as when I had first been allocated this place. The smell of stale ink reached my nostrils and I remembered the time I had tipped a whole bottle of ink over the desk making such a mess; I was in dire trouble. I walked slowly along the corridors remembering the laughter and shouts of the other children. But I sure wouldn't miss that Mr Porter, the teacher who always seemed to appear in the girls' changing rooms when we were to have showers after gym. His excuse was that it was his duty to make sure we were alright and didn't slip over. He was the teacher we needed to go to if we felt unwell. Why; did he always have to question whether 'it was that time of the month'?

Outside, I turned and looked back at the blue and white clad building. A chapter of my life had ended; reality dawned, no more school! This is it! I've made my escape! No goodbyes, I was free, and I smiled to myself as I walked out through the school gates and felt a huge weight lift from my shoulders.

My steps were light as I walked home along the streets so familiar to me; the semi-detached houses with their neat gardens running either side. As the road split into two, I stared at the corner plot nearest to me. Of course, that was the home of the midwife who delivered me. I pushed my short brown hair behind my ears and sighed. Yes; and it was she who named me too! My own mother couldn't think of what to call me so I ended up being named after two majestic liners.

Shrugging my shoulders, I walked on realising the enormity of what I had done; I was venturing out into the big wide world now and it was with some trepidation and heavy feet that I walked down the road and made my way down the front path. Opening the front door slowly, I went into the kitchen and made a much-needed cuppa! I was feeling really nervous about facing what was to come, I hadn't discussed what I'd planned with my parents but then I'd only decided when I was lying in bed the night before feeling there had to be something more exciting than school.

Mum's voice wove its way amongst the clutter in the hallway. "That you, Mary? Your father will be home in a minute and he's not going to like this electric bill that's arrived. I bet you've been using that electric fire in your room; I've heard him telling you on several occasions no more than an hour!"

I heard the front door squeaking open and Dad's voice calling out, "You got my tea on the table yet, Mother?"

My hands started shaking and I pinched myself to take my mind off what was to come. Gosh, what had I done? No: I knew best and had wanted to be out of that school for some months now. "Nice day at work, Dad?" I asked as he popped his head into the kitchen and grabbed my cuppa out of my hands without so much as a hello or thank you.

"You want a cuppa, Mum?" I called out. Hopefully, she didn't as I wanted to get this over with.

12

"I'd have told you if I wanted one, wouldn't I?" So, no came back to me.

Was this really me walking into the dining room? Was I really going to tell them what I'd done? "I've got something to tell you." I settle into the uneasy chair; a spring had gone long ago. There was a shake to my voice as I spoke. "Well, I... I... I... I've left school." You could slice through the heavy silence and both their jaws had sagged open. Were their eyes really protruding out of those aged sockets? Phew; I'm scared now and started shaking.

My father looked at me, he began to speak but Mum with one of her wild looks spread across her face started to shout, "You, stupid stupid girl…"

"Shut up, will you, you stupid woman, I'm dealing with this, you've no say in the matter!"

Mum huffed out of the room, slamming the door behind her leaving the rattling china to settle back into silence in the wall unit.

"Well, my girl what have you got to say for yourself?" There was definitely a hint of anger in his words.

I shifted in the chair trying to get off the broken spring that was sticking in my bum. "I just couldn't stand it anymore Dad, it was so boring, and yes it was a spur-of-the-moment thing; but it feels the right thing to have done."

He coughed and asked, "What did your form teacher say?"

*Keep calm girl*, I told myself. "They don't know yet, I didn't say anything, and you can't make me go back because I won't."

Strangely, it wasn't as bad as I feared, Dad thought it was good that I would be bringing in some money. When Mum

13

came back looking rather sheepish, she just said, "You might meet a nice boy and get married."

The getting married thing really bugged me. Since I was about fourteen, I'd heard it so often it had taken root in my mind. I'd come to realise that probably they wanted rid of me. When had I ever heard words of praise?

Dad's face to my mum conveyed a look of 'Don't say another word'. He, however, made her go and get a pile of local newspapers from the coal shed, and sent me upstairs with orders to search the job vacancy column in them.

I came up with one particular job I liked the look of; Office Junior, it was at a petrol station and car sales showroom in town. The next morning, I went to the phone box and rang the manager and was asked to go for an interview. I had a very strange excited scary feeling inside me.

Surprisingly, I coped with the interview apart from wriggling around on my chair and stammering a bit. He explained that among my tasks (making tea and filing the office paperwork), I would be learning how to use a Burroughs accountancy machine and be responsible for the garage customer accounts. I was really good with figures so it would be ideal. Oh, it all sounded so exciting!

A few days later, a letter arrived confirming my post as an 'Office Junior'. I felt the bees-knees when I told my parents I had got myself a good job and a salary of four pounds a week. Dad told me I would have to give Mum one pound a week, save one pound and use the rest for travelling and personal expenses. I had financial independence and although I would still be bound by time restrictions, it was very different to a school regime. What an achievement for a fifteen-year-old! I couldn't wait to start life as a working girl.

# Chapter 2
## *Here I Am*

I was so excited that I could hardly sit still on the bus. Me on a bus going to work, I had a job, yes me a working girl! By the time I neared the garage, I had butterflies fluttering around in my tummy. I was scared but who wouldn't be starting their first day of their first job and what a first day it was too.

I was sent to make the tea for the managing director's meeting. Boy, did the china clatter as I tentatively entered his domain? Thank goodness, I didn't have to pour and serve it; my hands shook so much I would have spilt it everywhere.

Phew! Back at my desk, I calmed down. *For goodness sake, Mary he's only a bloke, he sits on the toilet like all of us.* Now he was down to size, I could relax. My phone startled me as it started to ring. "Hello, Mary speaking."

"Mr Whiteman here," a loud condescending voice blasted my ear drum, "you haven't put the tea in the teapot! Would you sort it right now!"

Oh damn, blast, bloody hell. How could I be so stupid? I had been told I was just-a-nothing when I was young and they were right. I couldn't even make a pot of tea properly. Having retrieved the offending pot, my head hung in shame as rows of eyes followed me across the boardroom. With cheeks flamed crimson and feeling like a naughty schoolgirl, I went back to the kitchen and rather indignantly threw the tea bags in.

Muttering under my breath, I returned the said pot and fled before rebellious Mary stuck her tongue out in an act of defiance. Dashing past the door to the workshops, I failed to see one of the mechanics and of course, collided with him. He smelt all oily and his hands and face were streaked with dirt. A pair of twinkling, pale blue eyes stared at me. "Oh, oh sorry," I mumbled. Feeling a fool seemed to be the theme of the day.

The twinkly-eyed person spoke, "You obviously weren't looking, were you? Is something wrong? I thought you were in training for a marathon at the speed you were going."

"No, I'm fine," and I just stared at the blond wavy hair that hugged his head. I noticed his lip turned up at one corner as he spoke and all sense of reality seemed to be disappearing. I suddenly felt like I was floating, my eyesight went out of focus and I started coughing.

As quickly as he had appeared, he disappeared. The momentary sounds of clanging and banging, and engines being turned rushed in from the open workshop door and as it shut with a click the smell of petrol was left hanging in the air.

What eyes, what hair, and those overalls, they just seemed to cling to his slender form. White but covered in dirt, but oh so sexy. I was smitten big time. Daydreams, night dreams, fantasies and scenes of romance played out in my mind, I was love-sick.

One of my colleagues told me his name so I could lie in bed and allow my mouth to form his name on a tiny exhalation of breath, Philip. Oh, I felt all shivery. Here he was, Philip, my 'Knight in Shining Armour' I'd so longed for, oh thank you, my knight. I would be able to escape home, that place where I never felt wanted, where I felt they were trying to get rid of me.

That night as I lay curled up in bed, I pondered over some of my younger years; those heavy hands that slapped my legs as I raced up the stairs. Slap sting ouch, slap. Sobbing, my words spilling out all tangled up as I begged my dad to stop, "I'm sorry, I didn't mean to be a baddy girl, Ssooorry," as another rough hand connected with my tender skin. I'd clamber faster trying to escape the wrath of my dad as my mother screamed, "Do something about her, will you!!!"

So, he did. Very obedient was my dad where my mother was concerned. Yet he could be tender and gentle with me which only caused confusion in my young mind. Love meant hurt and pain and so the story went on.

There were those yearly holidays to the Saxona Guest House in Weston-super-Mare; whenever the son of the proprietor was around Mum would say, "Go on, there's one!" How the hell did I know what she was alluding to, it made no sense in my young mind.

My heart is heavy as I remember these things, of what I endured, of the emotions I suppressed, of the anger that was kept tight inside of me. Not just from those uncaring experiences but all of it, all the bloody lot. No love but an iceberg of a mum, an empty skeletal form devoid of all warmth for her daughter. For me, Mary, the innocent in all of this.

But now there was Philip. Ooh, it was so exciting. Gradually, I settled into my job and enjoyed the challenge. A

17

huge Burroughs accountancy machine which bucked and rattled through its daily routine was my buddy, I was nimble-fingered and felt confident as I pressed the keys and entered in the main the correct amounts. At last, I was beginning to feel a somebody, I felt more confident and had a focus in life.

Part of my daily workload was to fill the cigarette machines out on the forecourt and occasionally, Philip would saunter past, his clear blue eyes flickering into mine for a second or two. I called my reactions 'jelly leg' moments when the strength in my legs disappeared and they felt wobbly like a Chivers jelly.

My fantasies continued. The first kiss when his lips lightly brushed mine, his warm breath against my cheek, the smell of his aftershave wrapping itself around me making my head a little giddy. Then his slender hand cleaned of grease fingering my hair and the words, 'I love you' being sacredly whispered into my ear. Ooh, scrumptious...

Now he was saying hello to me. My knight was speaking to me, my saviour, my rescuer. The curl on his lip reminded me of Elvis, not that I was a fan of his. No, for me it was Cliff Richard, dreamy Cliff.

I was sent out to the workshop one day to check something out with the foreman. There was Philip, head under the bonnet of a Morris Minor, tinkering around with a spanner or some such tool. He looked up and our eyes locked together; it was as if there was an invisible beam between us. An electric current was flowing into me and my heart jumped and skipped erratically in my chest. Having sorted the queries with the foreman, Philip intercepted my return to the office. He looked quite shy now and shyness suddenly overcame me. My hand fumbled with my hair, twisting and pulling it in nervous anticipation.

"It's Mary, isn't it? How are you? I've noticed you about at times but we've never had a chance to chat."

My cheeks were well red by now and the 'jelly legs' had turned into 'wobbly, wobbly' legs.

I just looked at him, eyes wide, mouth gaping open. My brain had lost its entire vocabulary of words. Voiceless, I just gawked. Somehow, I managed a lip-trembling smile of sorts. A voice from what seemed like a distant shore gradually reached my ears, "How do you fancy coming out for a drink?"

*What, with you?* I muttered. *Of course, with bloody him, you twit,* a secondary voice bellowed in my head.

Putting his head to one side Philip said, "Well, there's no one else about is there?" And he grinned and looked around.

I'm sure I had been set up as all the other mechanics had disappeared and even the foreman was ensconced in his office. "Oh, um, um well um, I could," this other – Mary replied. I had dreamt of this moment for weeks, months. I'd thought of nothing else and now it was happening I'd turned into a mumbling, jumbling wreck.

Philip looked at me, his lop-sided grin spread over his face. It enhanced the six o'clock shadow, or was it the nine o'clock stubble?

Grinning back, feeling less of a prat, I looked into those opaque eyes and said, "Yes please!"

"Ok," and he visibly relaxed. "We'll arrange it tomorrow. Pop out to the workshop and we'll fix it up, I'm on lunch break at twelve-thirty."

I walked back to my desk on cloud nine, a lovely warmth filling me. Oh, my knight had asked me on a date! "Hey Pat, Philip's asked me out." I was glowing as I spoke.

"Well, thank goodness for that," she quipped, "Sitting facing a love-sick teenager is no fun, you know. Mooning around the office isn't any good for you. Men, they all end up letting you down and hurting you, but you'll find out."

I glowered at her and a burst of anger flew out, "Philip's not like that! He's a decent guy, you've only got to look at him." And slamming my ledger on the desk, I flounced out to the toilet to preen myself.

Having tossed and turned all night, I looked baggy-eyed when I arrived at work. Pat patched me up with some great foundation and even a smear of her new lipstick. She had a good heart really. As far as I knew, her husband had cheated on her and she had become very bitter about men. 'They can't be trusted' was her motto! It was a shame she'd let herself go. Her hair was a blonde frizz and she wore such old-fashioned clothes and that smudged red lipstick. Well really! Yet she was good to me and I began to see her as a mother figure. She had my best interest at heart. I was beginning to learn that it doesn't matter how someone looks it's about how they treat you and she treated me well.

And Gwen a young, happy-go-lucky person, down to earth and such fun to be around was all giggly and girly. "How exciting, – Mary. Young love and all that," and she blew kisses at me.

I felt the heat rush into my cheeks, "Oh, shut up, Gwen it's a first date, perhaps we'll get bored with each other."

"No, not you two," Pat piped up. "You can sense the electricity between you, high voltage that's what you two are."

"For goodness' sake, don't talk such rot," I said and bent my head and concentrated on my work.

Lunch time came and I found Philip sitting on an old wooden crate by the door to the yard catching a few rays of autumn sunshine. He was poking around in his sandwich tin and then taking bites out of his sarnies. Oh, how those luscious pink lips moved on the bread before his teeth, white and even, bit into it. He turned towards me, having heard the click of my heels on the concrete as I approached and waved, I glowed with anticipation.

"Come and join me, – Mary, I made a few extra sarnies. Here, have one. Now, how about Friday evening? I could pick you up at 7.30, what do you think?"

"That's fine with me," and I beamed at him, surprised my voice was so calm and clear. "Yes…yes." No more a dream but a happening event now; only two days to go, and then…

Luscious, scrumptious Friday came. Iceberg questioned me, but – Mary was evasive. No one, especially her, was going to spoil this momentous evening. The doorbell rang and I raced to answer it; I grinned at Phillip and joined him on the step, it was a two-person step after all. As I pulled the door to, Mum's screechy voice called out, "Mind what you get up to!"

What the hell was she on about now? Mums!

I know there was a huge smile on my face and a deep pink flush gracing my cheeks. He was in tight jeans and a loose checked shirt. Why am I noticing his clothes, and not looking at his face? It's because an embarrassed, shy timid little girl had taken me over. Oh! Raising my eyes, they met his, they

21

were so bright and alert. Everything seemed so familiar about his face now but it still made me catch my breath. I followed him up the path to his car aware hawk eye was behind the net curtains in the lounge watching my every move. Gosh, what a monster of a car it was too, all its edges were square.

What an evening! Dream-like I seemed to float through the time we spent together. A drive through twisting country lanes, autumnal colours gracing us along the way. The remnants of summer drifted by now, a chill in the air. But to me, it was all beautiful. I felt beautiful, but why wouldn't I, when I was with the man of my dreams, my Prince Charming, my rescuer? Dad would be pleased I had found someone to marry and I was only fifteen. I'd been a good girl to do as I was told, and Iceberg would be pleased to get rid of me. At last, someone to cuddle, to give me love, how amazing is that? And the little girl inside me sighed with relief.

We spent time in an old country pub, just talking about life in general. Sitting close, thighs touching, the warmth from his body seeping into mine. Mm-mm…how time flew. Before I knew it, I was at the end of the most amazing evening of my life. Why couldn't time stand still, why couldn't we be suspended in a bubble of timelessness? Why, oh why? My heart sank, knowing I would soon be back in that house, cold, dark, miserable, loveless and lonely.

Pulling up outside the house, number thirteen would you believe, a number thought to be unlucky. Philip turned and took my hand. As a shiver rippled through me, I grinned like a Cheshire cat. He looked at me quizzically, then leaned closer and his hot breath tickled my neck then my cheeks. His lips were slightly parted and ever so gently he brushed them against mine. Heat flared up my face, trembling began in my legs; it felt as if I had turned a somersault.

I looked into his eyes, mine wide in wonderment, and as he gazed back, I noticed his breathing had changed—it had quickened and deepened. Squeezing my hand, he said. "Would you like to come out tomorrow? There's a great folksy group playing at one of the pubs in town."

"I'd really like that, Philip," and smiling I slid from my seat to stand on the pavement looking lost as he drove away. His facial features were implanted clearly into my young mind, I could never think of them disappearing.

The house was in darkness, thank goodness for that, they'd obviously gone to bed and I grappled for the key which hung on a piece of string behind the letter box. I glowed inside. I'd never felt this way before and I liked it. Long may it last! Now that was a funny thing to say, wasn't it? As I made my way up the stairs a voice yelled out, "That you, Mary?"

Who the bloody hell does she think it is? "Yes, Mum, it's me," I replied with as much patience as I could.

Climbing into bed and sinking beneath the cool sheets, I breathed deeply and drifted into a dreamless sleep. The last thing I remember thinking about was the touch of his gentle hand on mine, it filled me with hope.

A *touch so soft and gentle*
*a whisper of hope*
*silence, stillness and peace*
*caresses the air we breathe.*

# Chapter 3
## *Softening into Bliss*

So began the journey with my beloved, someone who claimed a part of my heart. Although I was not aware this had happened until a torrent of emotions rushed out of me and I began to realise that this relationship, in fact, the whole experience with him was changing the course of my life. Philip was my friend, a companion, a beautiful young man who graced my life and who showed me love. His mates had a nickname for him, 'Chet'. Phillip was a great fan of Chet Atkins the musician and was always going on about him.

Those evenings out together when lips to lips created delicious thrills to race through my whole body meant so much. It seemed as if a heat moved up and down my spine, tingling sensations raced through my fingers and I felt as though I was being lifted off the ground. Everything seemed more alive around me, colours appeared more vibrant. Feeling those sensations course around my body soothed me, I let go and relaxed into love.

Oh, the joy of hands connecting. Gentle touches, hugs and cuddles as days were spent in the countryside and evenings in cosy old pubs with log fires crackling in huge fireplaces. There were snatched looks of sacred love at work that brightened my day, lit up my life. My darling I love you, but what did I know of love at fifteen?

Time was spent in our parents' homes, but precious to my heart were the times we spent alone: cocooned in our own sacred bubble of time. My life had changed I could see a future now beyond all that had been.

One cold winter's night at my parents' house, Philip suggested we snuggle up on my bed. His hand took mine, his skin felt soft and slightly moist; nothing was spoken, in silence, he led me slowly up the stairs. I just went quiet and obediently I did as he suggested.

A strange feeling came over me. Somewhere in the recesses of my mind, a memory tried to find a pathway to remind me of a past event but other than this peculiarity in my body nothing was remembered.

To lie side by side fully clothed with my beloved was beautiful, I felt so safe being held. Then somehow yet again a strange feeling began to take me over and I felt as though I was outside of myself and experiencing it all through a swirling mist.

A hand moved to different parts of my body making gentle stroking motions; I was experiencing weird sensations which I'd never felt before. Then his body moved over me making strange movements. I didn't feel any discomfort just this rhythm as he moved slowly then a bit faster. His breathing deepened and then a deep groan. I couldn't understand what was happening. It must be something like a different type of kiss. A special kiss! How weird. Can you kiss with another part of your body? Do we have another set of lips? I was very confused! Oh, my goodness he's weeing on me and I felt my face redden and glow.

25

I was shaking now and my voice came out like a scratchy, inaudible mumble. "Phillip, what have you been doing? I don't understand."

"Shush," he replied in soft tones, "I love you, Mary, I was just being loving to you that's all," and he kissed me tenderly.

My heart flipped and then raced, he loved me, loved me he'd never told me that before. I turned and glanced into those cool blue eyes and spoke gentle words of love. "My love for you, Philip, is from a deep place within me, I'll love you forever." Then I cried softly into his shoulder.

I was startled by the sound of the front door opening, the familiar sound of its groans trailed up the stairs. It always stuck and you had to give it a hefty push until it shot open. No matter how you tried to gauge it there was always an element of surprise when it gave way.

"You there, Sis?" And I realised that my brother had come home. He was supposed to be at a skittle match until late; what the hell was he doing back so early?

Philip jumped up, and fumbling with his clothes, he rushed downstairs. I heard voices and the sound of the front door closing. Footsteps echoed up the front path and the sound of a car door opening and then slamming shut startled me.

I desperately needed to wee and rushed to the toilet; strange what special kissing does to you, all a bit messy too! Where did all this sticky stuff come from? I found Philip downstairs and he explained that my brother had come back to ask us to go and play skittles, so off we went. But I still felt strange. Distant memories were trying to echo through the years but didn't quite make it. I shook my head as if the movement would free something up. Nothing!

The weeks went on and we never did the special kiss thing again. Obviously, it wasn't so special after all, my Prince Charming never mentioned anything about it.

# Chapter 4
## *The Bug*

Work was going well; I was so happy. Phillip provided comfort and I felt so safe in his arms. The bad days had gone now, life was exciting and the future for us I felt was sealed. And then I caught some stupid bug. Mornings were the worst, when I would retch and heave and strange-looking yellow stuff would be spat into the cracked wash basin. I got to know every one of those cracks and the patterns they made. Thank goodness no one in the household seemed to notice. Oh well. Pat had told me there had been a bout of strange bilious attacks going around so I felt reassured.

Still, I continued to feel queasy and to add to it all, it upset that special time of the month; I must be really out of sorts. Strangely, I didn't say anything to Philip, maybe he wouldn't like me if I told him I was unwell? Perhaps he was the sort of person that didn't like sickness?

Pat started looking at me strangely. Her mouth would open as if she was going to say something but then she'd close it quickly and go back to her work. Once I caught her and Gwen whispering in the corridor. Probably they had something personal to discuss.

I was retching in the toilet one day at work when Pat came in, "Seems like you've got yourself in a fix, Mary!"

"I'm not sure what you mean, Pat. It's this damn bug I can't seem to shake it off, my system is being really upset by it."

"You should go and see your doctor, Mary," and she patted my arm. "You're so young to be having a baby."

"Jesus Christ, having a baby! You're joking! I don't find that funny, Pat. It's a bug."

Pat stared at me, "I'll be buggered if it's a bug, my girl, you're having a baby, Philip's been and got you in the family way. Didn't you take precautions?"

"Precautions?" I exclaimed. "What the hell are you going on about precautions for?"

"Well, Johnnies then, you know," her voice sounded terse.

"Johnnies. Who the bloody hell is that? I don't know any Johnnies," I shouted.

Pat stared at me; she looked a bit perplexed. "Well, French letters."

"Look, I bloody well can't speak or write French. What has a stupid letter got to do with this bug I've caught?"

She dropped her arms to her side in frustration and went on, "You've caught all right, girl and it's no bug! You're pregnant. You're going to have a baby. A BABY!"

My head spun, I heaved, retched and started sweating. "A baby, a baby? But how did a baby get inside me? How did I get a baby?"

"Sex," she said.

"Sex," I replied.

"What's that?"

"Blimey, didn't your mum tell you anything?"

"Anything what?" I asked hysterically.

"You know, *IT*!"

"*IT*! What's *IT*?" And I stared at her helplessly.

"Bloody hell," and Pat came and hugged me. "You didn't know, did you?"

"Know what, for Christ's sake, Pat," I yelled. I looked at her with tears streaming down my face, I was trembling now. "Well, we did have a different sort of kiss, you know one of those special ones?"

Pat's mouth fell open, "A different sort of kiss, a special kiss?" Pat yelled. "That wasn't a special kiss, that was sex."

"Sex!" I exclaimed. "Sex?"

And Pat went on to explain what sex was and when she mentioned 'sticky stuff', all the blood drained from my head, I felt I was sinking. Oh, what had my knight done to me? My world disintegrated as I slumped to the floor.

Mumbling now I looked at her, fear raging through me. "You said it would hurt, well it didn't hurt, there was no blood. Well, I suppose there was a lot of sticky stuff and now I think about it there was a bit of a fishy smell."

Pat put her hands on her hips, "Sticky stuff, smelt like fish? That's sperm, that's what makes babies and it only took one sperm to make yours."

I was going to have a baby, and shame appeared like a huge, ugly monster and gobbled me up. I felt like a rough grain of sand on a beach with gigantic waves crashing over me pounding me deep into the shore. I was gasping for breath as my heart pounded rapidly in my chest. Suddenly a stinging sensation flooded my cheek and as I looked through foggy eyes, I saw Pat's hand flaying in the air. She'd slapped my face.

My nightmare life that I thought had ended now took on a new blacker nightmarish experience.

The GP I saw said I was very unlucky to get caught the first time. He offered to tell my parents, and as he said it, I could see he felt sorry for me. He knew Mum well.

Of course, I had to tell Phillip and he didn't seem at all concerned, he didn't panic he went and got me some gin and told me to sit in a hot bath and drink it. Sipping the awful liquid neat from the bottle made me feel even sicker and all I ended up with was a blinding headache. I was terrified my parents would find the empty bottle. Mind you, I thought Philip was a bit miserly, it was only a quarter bottle he got for me. I felt so terribly alone, so scared. What would happen next?

Iceberg with her hawk eyes obviously realised something was amiss. The coal-burning stove in the kitchen hadn't been receiving its monthly presents from me. She challenged me. "Are you going to have a baby, Mary?" Her scratchy voice threw the words at me while her face contorted in various nasty-looking expressions, her lips were pursed and puckered. Glowering at me, she repeated the question, "Are you going to have a baby?" And before I could answer she snarled and said, "You are, aren't you? I knew it! You stupid, stupid girl. I kept telling you mind what you get up to! Glory be," and she paced up and down waving her arms about like some demented person muttering all sorts of incantations I could make no sense of.

"What will the neighbours say? Oh my gawd, I'll never be able to face them again. See what you've brought on me." On and on she went.

Her words came at me like a volley of balls being smashed around on a tennis court. I sensed the evil at that moment. She stormed into the hall screaming, "She's bloody well going to have a baby. Do you hear? A baby! Oh my gawd, the neighbours!"

She raced back, Dad trailing behind her, his face white. I could see his clenched fists. That spelt real trouble. Off she went again, saliva splattering from her mouth, "You'll have to get rid of it! Crochet hook, knitting needle or something."

Now it was his turn, fist raised, he subjected me to a torrent of abuse, getting more and more wound up as he shouted, "After all we've done for you, you go and do this. You ungrateful girl. You can't keep it; you'll have to give it away. Does Philip know? I suppose you'll say it's his fault. I know you, my girl, you've always stirred things up!"

I cowered against the wall, shaking, wanting to be somewhere else but here in this room with them. He looked at me as if I was dirt. Visibly shaking with anger, he blasted me again, "You slut, you disgusting thing," and hit me to the floor and kicked me as I lay there stupefied. But my mind was still able to ponder how on earth could this short, skinny man—be so aggressive, so nasty, so horrible?

All I wanted to do was die, what a relief that would have been. But my brother appeared and intervened. I staggered to my room devoid of all hope, desperately ashamed and although my body moved, another Mary followed behind, disconnected, numbed and feeling so lost.

It was like an octopus's tentacles latching onto me; my life force was being sucked out. Fear yet again became my companion. I was still that 'nothing'. Those words had been well and truly planted in my young self all those years ago,

32

and I just can't bring myself to say who had told me I was just a nothing!

I tried telling them I didn't know what had happened, that I'd had what I thought was a special kiss.

"Special kiss, special kiss. Just listen to what rubbish she's talking," and my dad turned to my mother in frustration. "The girl's mental, we should have had her put in a home years ago just like you kept telling me, but I never listened, did I? We wouldn't be in this mess now for sure."

I stood there open-mouthed, my brain trying to make sense of it all. Not only had my dad bruised me physically but I felt traumatised emotionally and psychologically. So, this is what love is my young mind thought. What Philip and my dad had set up for me was an equation of what love consisted of. Men + abuse + pain + sexual contact = relationships = love. Isn't that all a bit crazy, a deadly recipe for disaster for sure. How could my mind have such clarity—at a time like this?

# Chapter 5
## *Influences*

I'm here now in this dark place with both sets of parents arguing and accusations being thrown backwards and forwards. My knight, who for me had fallen from grace, just stood there expressionless. I'd received the thrust of his lance and that had been bittersweet.

At one gathering of the parents, Philip looked very upset and came to me and before I could say anything, he was asking me to marry him. He'd gently placed his arm around me and looked into my eyes, there seemed to be a gentle pleading. There was no electricity now, only anguish as our eyes flickered again in momentary contact. The light had gone out, but it was a noble gesture he made.

"Philip, yes I'll marry you," and my heart sang. "Oh yes, please, it will work out, you'll see." We touched. A slight flame being rekindled. My body began to relax a little and warmth was gently seeping through me.

"We're getting married," we shouted in unison. "It will be fine now, so don't worry."

Four pairs of eyes aghast at our revelation swivelled onto us. "Married?" They chorused. "Don't be so bloody stupid!

That's crazy! You're too young! It will never work!" Their voices became a cacophony of harsh retorts.

I died once more and my eyes dropped to the floor, a heavy heart within me again. Philip and I stepped away from each other, hopelessness and despair now our only connection in that moment. Our protestations fell on deaf ears. They didn't care about us, only themselves.

"We're contacting Social Services," Mum yelled. "You were underage at fifteen, it's a criminal offence." Philip's face went white; his parents winced.

"No!" I yelled. "No!"

A despairing look passed between my fallen knight and me as he left with his parents. You could feel the tension in the air as they turned and looked at me with disgust, I knew they were blaming me, I could sense it. What's new I thought everyone has always blamed me since I was little, I've been the scapegoat for so many. Life's not fair.

But I had no choice in what was to happen next, they just took over. I was a bystander when in reality I should have been the main character. The spotlight though shone on them and I was cast to the sidelines.

Voices raged; decisions were cast in tablets of stone. "You're going in a home, Mary, one for unmarried mothers. You'll give up the baby, you can't keep it. You've brought shame on us. And the neighbours! What will they say?" Mum screeched. "That bloody busy-body at number twelve will love getting her teeth into this, it will be all around the village in no time. You mark my word!"

"But, but I… I…"

"Shut up, you've no choice," Dad said. "It's settled."

How many times can you survive falling into a blackening abyss? A place where you can't breathe and hundreds of dark, ugly hands grab at you trying to drag you even further into hell. Let me die, let me be dead and done with this life. But my prayers went unanswered.

Social Services booked me into St Catherine's, St C's for short, an unmarried mothers' home in a nearby town. How many other girls will be there I wondered? How many are as scared as me at what would be happening to them and their babies? Are they wondering just like me where our babies will go? Would they be constantly looking in prams, then pushchairs and glancing at little ones toddling, walking, wondering, watching children down through the years, could that be my child? Maybe? Of course not! Would I and the other mums who were there go on to have other children? Would we all suffer and have regrets and never have happiness in our lives again?

Are they feeling—just like me? Emotionally switched off, detached, dead in a sense, going through the motions of life. But there are other Marys that walk alongside me, still connected in some way as though an invisible energy cord kept them nearby. But now, down the years, they are being lovingly welcomed back. Sadly, with this welcoming comes the pain too. The shame, the fear, the sadness, the betrayal and the anger. The whole bloody lot comes to be dealt with. But it has to be this way as all is for healing. I've found courage, been brave. At times I run, at times I stuff food, and drink to comfort the suffering – Mary. However, it's pushing me to be made free. No one else can do it, only me, with help from others now along the way.

It took me into my sixties before I could say I have three children, not two as I have stated down the years, living a lie, but three and I love them all and along with this love comes a multitude of other emotions that go with being a parent.

It's strange, or maybe not so, but I can't remember if I saw my beloved much after the furore of that evening when the clan gathered. I remember Mum saying once, "Don't bring her home late." So, I obviously did meet up with him again. For what reason I have no idea and what passed between us, I have no recollection of.

People at work were kind. Once Gwen asked me if she could measure me as a friend of hers was pregnant and she wanted to make her a couple of maternity dresses. A few months later she presented me with the dresses. I'd never guessed and cried when this act of kindness was shown to me.

Did I see Philip around at work? Alas, I have no memory recall of seeing him there but I'm sure I must have done. Or maybe he kept a low-key profile? Avoiding me like the plague.

I did a foolish thing and that was giving up my job at the garage in the later stages of my pregnancy. No one said, "I could go back." I have no idea whether they had maternity leave in those days and my boss never spoke to me about it. And what about Philip? Having him around, would that not have caused me much embarrassment and pain? There would have been a constant reminder of all that had happened and what if I heard on the grapevine he had a new love; the thought of it was unbearable.

# Chapter 6
## *The House of Shame*

Eventually, the time came for my incarceration in St C's. What a place! A spinster of a woman was in charge with no idea of the emotional turmoil we girls were going through. Counselling and support weren't things that society was pre-disposed to. How can anyone in their right mind stick you in a home and get you to look after your baby for six weeks and then take it away from you? For Christ's sake, how cruel is that? The bastards! And what of the effect on the baby—the bonding and all that?

I loved the cook at St C's. She was a homely woman and she used to laugh in a kindly way when I had seconds of plums and custard, my favourite dessert. The rich creamy custard comforted me in some way, it was so yummy. Thank you, kind woman, you brought a little warmth into my life. Amazing…

We were unpaid skivvies at St C's, cleaning, dusting, scrubbing. It wasn't much fun for the 'big belly' brigade. There were some nice girls there though, and we did what we could to support each other. Girls would come and go. It was agonising when mums were separated from their babies. There were enough tears shed there to fill an ocean.

My brother got married during my term at St C's. He'd been another one to judge and rubbish me. How dare he after what he tried to do to me as a child, and the threats that followed. They did allow me to go to the wedding although my bump was large now. I felt so ashamed and thought everyone was looking at me. I wore a silky, orange pleated dress—it must have looked gross; I would have been a bridesmaid but I mucked that up, didn't I?

I really slammed into my mother when she came to visit one day, she'd forgotten the dress I was to wear at the wedding. I bullied her until she went all the way home to collect it. Eleven miles there and back and a mile walk to bus stops each way. I felt so guilty about how I treated her that day, I was like a demanding child wanting her way. I wonder if she ever felt guilty about how she was to me when I was little. In me lay such deep anger, how could she be so callous, where was her understanding, love and support throughout my younger days?

I felt so ashamed and guilty about how I had behaved. But I managed to be a little kind to myself, after all, look at the situation I was in, the most horrible of horrible there could ever be.

Sally, my sister-in-law, was great. She felt Philip and I should have been allowed to get married; well live together until we could. "I'm sure you would have made a go of it," she told me. Who knows? It's too late now, isn't it?

Well, poor Mary had high blood pressure and I had to go into hospital for bed rest. The matron of St C's wasn't too pleased. I was after all the lackey that cleaned her rooms, and they were so much more palatial than ours for sure. I remember her moaning that I had left some dust on her dresser one day. My reply rather cheekily was, "Well, when you vacuum, the dust rises up and has to settle somewhere."

"Well, vacuum first and dust after," was her retort; and she rolled those eyes that lacked any warmth at me. A relation of my mum's perhaps?

A few days after my admission to St Paul's Maternity Hospital for bed rest, they broke my waters. It seemed like gallons splashed to the floor, probably not as much as I thought but it did make quite a noise and the medics looked surprised. I felt very vulnerable with my legs strapped up in these stirrup-like things, so embarrassingly horrible.

And then it began—the terror of all terrors. The pain started straight away; I was so scared. A nurse sat with me in a side room and I remember thrashing around yelling, "Why the hell did I do it?" *'IT'… 'IT'… 'IT'… 'IT'…* Why?

\* \* \* \*

I'd never seen Philip since being incarcerated in the home. How I longed for him to be there, to rescue me from this terrifying experience. Yet he was the bastard who put me in this position. Didn't he think about the consequences of what he was doing? Why didn't he have one of those things that Pat had gone on about, or a 'willie helmet' someone had once said to me? Or maybe he just got carried away in the moment. I don't think so—after all, he had led me upstairs, so he knew his intention.

Well, he should have been more controlled, after all, he was three years older than me. I was fifteen and, emotionally the age of a much younger child.

\* \* \* \*

The pain now was excruciating. It felt as if millions of daggers were being stuck into my stomach, and a vice-like grip was wrapping around my swollen abdomen. It was hell!

They transferred me into what looked like an operating theatre. I remember the glinting eyes peering at me over the tops of masks. There seemed to be a lot of commotion happening everywhere. Lights beamed down at me, but it was soft, not dazzling. Rattles, clatters, bustling and whispered voices came at me through a fog. I felt bemused as to what was going on. Strange smells filtered into my nostrils; I didn't like them one bit. And before I knew it needles were being stuck into my arm; a pair of eyes loomed closer and a funny-shaped mask held in smelly gloved hands was pressed over my face. A discarnate voice told me to breathe deeply and everything gradually drifted away, the sounds became muffled and then nothingness engulfed me.

Yet again, no one told me what was happening to me, to my body. Why do people never ask permission to touch my body? Who do they think they are that they can just do it? As the fog of the smelly stuff started to lift, a flashing picture came clearly into my mind. I was in a stable and this old farmer type person was close to me. He took my hand and shoved it in his dirty, tatty trouser pocket. I forced it back out; a warm fleshy thing had touched my fingers and I didn't like it. Terrified, I noticed there was a wooden pole extending out at the bottom of his filthy trousers which were tied with coarse string. His face was full of ruts and thin tight lips smirked, his eyes were bulbous and he had a stench of horse shit about him. I tried to back out through the stable door but he pushed me down on a rough mattress and threw himself onto me. Screaming, I began kicking and thrashing around until I freed

41

myself from his ghastly body and raced out the door, grabbed my bike and shot off at breakneck speed down the lane.

Suddenly, my eyes shot open; sweat was pouring off me and I thrashed and groaned around. A nurse held my hand and calmed me down reassuring me that everything was alright. My hand crept to my belly and I discovered my lump was gone. There was just this floppy mass of loose skin hanging. The pain was excruciating—you know, 'down there'. They'd had to cut me extensively to carry out a forceps delivery while I was under the anaesthetic. I could hardly move and felt faint. "Where's…where's the baby?" I choked.

"He's in special care," a warm happy-faced nurse told me.
I stared wide-eyed.

"His head's a bit bruised from his delivery. He was a big boy—nearly nine pounds. So, they're taking extra care of him. He'll be fine," and she patted my hand.

At this display of affection, I dissolved into tears.

"Don't worry, love, it's normal, you've been through a difficult time." She smiled, trying to reassure me as she spoke.

Difficult time! You can say that again, and I turned away and dissolved into uncontrollable sobbing; the nurse quietly left the room.

"Poor baby, you look so pale." I stood wobbling around on my weak legs; excruciating burning in a part of my body I never wanted touched again. "Poor, poor baby. What a pallid complexion you have and what have they done to your head?" A large bump stood out from his skull, bruises already appearing. He was still, just lying there inside his incubator as if in shock.

*Don't look in his eyes Mary, don't open your heart, keep detached. Don't, whatever you do, allow any feelings to flow*

42

*between you*. I stared at him, love stirring in my heart. I quickly snapped a padlock on it, turned and hobbled away, the physical pain in my body reminding me of the emotional pain I so carefully kept under lock and key.

Mum was in tears; someone must have called her. She was really playing on the drama of how I'd brought it all on myself and shame on the family. She gave an Oscar-winning performance. A drama queen, yeah that's what she was and guess who'd already become her understudy. Yes me!

I don't remember seeing Dad at the hospital and he certainly didn't come to St C's. Mum did though. It was something I appreciated, especially when she didn't harp on about what had happened. Why couldn't they see that I was innocent, that I'd been taken advantage of? What blinkered views people have of situations. Perhaps Philip had too thought all of this? Alas, I don't know, and probably never will. Maybe the universe will bring into play some synchronicity and our paths will cross again. What strange things my young mind came up with.

The days slipped by and I fed my son, changed his nappies and tended to all his needs. He loved his bottles and he would drink greedily resulting in lots of air being sucked in but thankfully he was great at burping. Night-time was the worst when I had to crawl from a warm bed to feed him when really all I wanted to do was disappear into a dark hole and never come out again. This bundle of flesh and blood was alive a heartbeat within him. His lungs drew in life-giving air, all that he was had made him into this little vulnerable person. But apart from the daring moments when I allowed a little love to creep out, I otherwise stayed detached. Poor us.

'Herr' matron didn't like the name I'd chosen. "Shane?" she said and looked at me with disapproval clearly visible in her eyes.

But what did I care? Time slipped by; I conjured up this fantasy, a fantasy about Phillip coming to see us. We would look at our son together and realise he was a miracle that we had given life to. Hope would stir, perhaps, just maybe we could survive this and somehow the three of us could build a life together. After all fairy tales have happy endings, the princess always got her prince, everything always turned out all right. Didn't it?

Life went on and then one day, Philip appeared. My fallen knight stood there looking solemn. There was no electricity between us, the spark had gone. The light had dimmed, the flames of love had flickered and died. Or was it just masked by the chain of events? Somehow both of us had had to survive through this ordeal, but I was for sure worse off.

Oh pain, oh sadness, now you are my constant companion. I felt I was going through a living death; 'A dark night of the soul' is an expression I have heard and I think it relates very well to what had been and what was happening.

Philip made eye contact; his blue eyes just stared into mine. Nothingness looked back from mine, a vacant lot now where love had once shone brightly into the world. There was no fluttering of my heart, no excitement flowing through me. All the vibrancy had gone I felt stiff like the trunk of a tree.

"Come and see your son, Philip," and I paused, but I started to shake and feel so cold. I took him to the pram shed where Shane lay peacefully in a black and white Silver Cross pram. It was huge and although he had been a hefty weight at birth, he looked lost in this monstrous wheeled machine. I suddenly realised I could feel the attraction to Phillip, the golden thread of love that had drawn us together was still there. Our eyes made contact just for a fraction of a second. My heart opened suddenly, like a partly budded rose that had been bathed in sunlight and suddenly in all its glory, parted its leaves in splendorous beauty releasing its fragrance.

Then to my horror, each petal darkened, shrivelled and fell away. Our love I knew, was doomed. How I wanted to reach out and touch him, feel that familiar smell next to me and breathe in the memories of our time together. But I didn't dare. I couldn't. These were memories, and I had to deal with what was happening right now. With a voice that seemed to come from another person's mouth, I mumbled, "Here, I'll pick him up, you can have a cuddle. He looks so much like you."

Phillip's expression changed, there seemed to be a lockdown happening to him. His lips were tight and his eyes held a distant look, his whole body seemed to stiffen and the connection I'd been feeling disappeared. I was suddenly feeling nervous, alone and scared. I had envisaged our reunion being so wonderful, so happy and hoped it would dawn on him that he couldn't let this happen, that his son needed him, I needed him, that we would be together forever and ever…

His eyes locked into mine and he replied in a serious tone, "No, no, I don't want to. It's too painful, I'll get upset," and averting his eyes he looked down at his feet.

"Too painful!" I cried. "Too bloody painful! What do you know of pain? I'm having to look after him every day. In the stillness of the night, I sit holding him, hearing the suck of his mouth drawing the warmth of the milk into his body. The heat of his little self against mine all the time, knowing that one day there will be emptiness in my arms where he lay. A space that will never be filled. Yes, what do you know of pain?"

The anger rose and I lashed out. "You don't want to see your son; what sort of person are you? You got me into this, you did this to me. Do you know what I've been going through? The shame I feel, the anguish that eats away at me night and day. Go away, just go away, it's all too much, I can't cope with it."

And he did, he just turned and walked out of my life. Never to be glimpsed again, or the sound of his voice penetrate my ears. My knight had fled; I had thought him brave but he was weak. Don't knights fight for their maidens? I had given him more than my handkerchief. He had taken so much but wasn't prepared to honour his responsibilities.

Perhaps if I'd been more mature, not in a place of dread at parting from my little one, or still suffering from the effects of the traumatic birth I might have handled it differently, but this is how it was. But I must be kind to myself, not burden myself with blame. All this longing I'd had to meet up with Phillip, to see how I felt after all this time, but what good has that done? My thinking had all been wrong, twisted, unreal; he didn't even apologise to me, or tell me he regretted being so unkind, that he felt ashamed of taking advantage of me, but hey ho that never happened. Of course, as I've mentioned before I'd been looking for that fairy tale ending; the prince finding his princess and living happily ever after. How immature I was to even think these things.

No one will ever understand or know how in that moment of his leaving, Mary died a million deaths. Another Mary stepped outside of herself and joined those already there. Soon I'll be an empty shell, devoid of emotion, every ounce of feeling, numb. Help me God to get through this, someone help me, please.

I stood alone and with a deep sigh walked back into the house to start the 'light duties' I'd been given. Due to the severity of the effects of the birth on my young body, I wasn't allowed to do the heavy work. Poor Mary, how she so wanted comfort. 'Light duties', you may ask, were scrubbing flights of stairs and flagstones down in the basement—light duties. As I knelt and scrubbed the floor backwards and forwards, my nails scraping the hard stone when the brush escaped my grasp, I let the tears fall and scrubbed at them roughly until they were obliterated cracking my nails until they bled.

A few days later, one of the girls came and told me I had been summoned by Herr Matron. I entered her office with trepidation. She looked up frowning, clearing her throat before she spoke. 'Mary, just to let you know, that arrangements have been made for er...' and she coughed loudly before speaking his name, 'er... Shane to be placed in a nursery.'

My head shot up and I gawped. 'But I thought he was going to be collected here by his new parents, like the other babies have been?'

'Well that's what's been decided and you'll be told a few days before he has to go so arrangements can be finalised about taking him there. The social worker will come and see you soon to explain.'

So matter-of-fact, so cold, not an ounce of compassion, not a flicker of warmth in her eyes.

Tears welled up and mumbling I started to ask, 'How...?''

She looked down at her papers and raised her hand in a dismissive gesture. I left feeling shaken and perturbed about what would happen now.

Back in the nursery, I looked down at my son and all I could feel was sorrow. That special kiss moment drastically changed the course of my life creating so much pain and unhappiness not just for me but for many people. My heart felt broken. "I'm so sorry, my darling, there's nothing I can do you see." But there was something I could have done! Fought for him, fought and fought to keep him. But did I stand up to those grown-ups who thought they knew best? No! I felt numb and helpless. They exerted their power over me thinking they knew best. They had no idea of the damage inflicted on all of these unmarried mothers here, with their determination to have the babies put up for adoption. I'd heard so much about this. Lots of gossip flew around the house. I can see it was a trend. Pregnant girls in homes having babies taken from them for adoption. Words still chattered in my mind, "It's best for the baby, you're too young, you won't cope." Blah blah blah along with a multitude of other – remarks said to me.

I need to be kind to Mary though. I was very immature and all that had happened to me had left me feeling helpless; I was after all just a child.

Although at times, part of me seemed to be operating from the place of an immature, vulnerable child, there is the other part whose mind has clear rational thinking. So grown up. It's almost as if I am another person, a wise woman. How can that be? It's like I've seen the future but then am back here in this moment. Would the course of life be that young, pregnant single girls would never appear shamed or hang their heads afraid of what folks might say, or how they would react to them? No being incarcerated in an unmarried mothers home. No pressure to give their babies up. Would they understand

48

how lucky they are, how easy they've had it? Although I am sure there would still be those who would have it tough for whatever reasons. I just sensed it couldn't go on this way, this horrible reaction of society, family and friends. Would they know of the consequences of doing a special kiss, the '*IT*', without using protection? That could result in them being-up-the-duff so to speak.

I cannot comprehend that this persecution, judgement and the cruelty of how I and others are being treated will continue.

\* \* \* \*

The dreaded day came closer and closer for me to leave the home, a bittersweet experience. Of course, I had tried to detach myself from Shane, but however hard I tried, it was impossible to stay totally devoid of feelings. I knew I was preparing myself for the known outcome of this situation. That he would never stay a part of my life, that I would never see him grow, toddle, cut his first tooth, start school, or become a man. There are so many firsts that I would miss out on. I do so hope he will be happy wherever he goes; that life is kind to him.

It had been decided, not by me of course but 'they', the deciders of mine and Shane's fate, that he would be placed in a nursery in Bristol. All I could do was go along with it. Dad had gone on to tell me yet again, he would never have me at home with a baby and where did an unmarried mum of sixteen go?

And then it was the day, that fateful day. That time that all the mums in St C's dreaded coming, but it came eventually for all of us. Oh, how sore my heart was, I cried inside but looked cold and calm to the world. The barriers were up and it had to stay that way for me to stay sane; devoid of feelings, detached, empty like a dried-up oasis.

# Chapter 7
## *The Nursery and Nearly Gone*

The day of leaving the unmarried mothers' home came. The six weeks since my baby was born had seemed like six days. Against all protocol, dad insisted we take him to the nursery ourselves.

I moved in a dreamlike state as though everything around me wasn't real. My head whirled with all the things that had been said to me by others: a lady from social services, my parents and the matron here at the home. The badgering, the constant undermining. I wasn't worthy to have my baby, I wasn't worthy to even be alive. It was hopeless to protest – they knew best! Or did they?

But I knew one thing: I was taking my baby to this place, this nursery. I'd have a little more time with him, a few more cuddles before…

Standing alongside Dad's car, my stomach churned. I faltered, wanting to run away with Shane. Suddenly Dad's voice cut through my thoughts. "Right, are you ready Mary?" He called. "We can't mess about; it's a long way to get to that place. Get a move on will you, and stop that damn baby caterwauling. Why the bloody hell, you had to go and get yourself pregnant I'll never know. You've disgraced us."

I braced myself, looked into his face and retorted, "Well, you should damn well speak to Philip about it; he was the one that did this to me. When have you ever had a go at him? Picking on me eh? A woman. Perhaps you're scared of him and his parents?"

Then my mother joined in, she had that horrible cold look on her face and her lips were twitching. "I don't know what the neighbours will think about all this, they'll be gossiping like hell, and that Mrs Jones at number forty-six will be the worst. Oh, and then there's that stupid woman at number twelve, common as muck she is with all the rollers in her hair."

My father's voice cut in, "For Christ's sake, woman, will you stop going on about the neighbours, especially that woman at number twelve, that's all you think about. If she's that bad, why do you go to Bingo with her? I reckon you like being one of her cronies."

Mum picked up her thread again, her voice was tight and croaky, "You're a stupid girl causing us all this trouble. When I think about all what we've done for you: given you a warm home, put up with your moods and tantrums and this is what you do to us."

Dad interrupted again, his tone was edged with rancour. "Shut up, will you! Mary, get that baby and get in the car right now!" At last, we were off. Shane cradled in my arms his bag of clothes stowed safely in the boot, the name labels neatly stitched to each item. Another inmate had kept an eye on Shane while I'd popped to the shops to buy him some clothes. Amazingly, my mother had given him a few things, something I never really understood. At least, he wasn't going to the nursery like a foundling left in a phone box or on

52

someone's doorstep. He was going to be safe, warm and looked after.

Of course, being a baby, he started crying again which didn't please my dad at all. "Shut him up, will you? I can't concentrate on my driving. I don't know why you didn't get someone else to drive you, we've had enough bloody stress over all of this as it is!"

"There was Dad! But you were the one that insisted on taking us!"

"Your bloody mother nagged me into it. I'd much rather have been out in the garden on a nice day like this. Those seed potatoes needed going in and I haven't sown the carrots yet, they should have been in last week."

He went on moaning and groaning and I just shut my ears to it all. Then Shane did the unthinkable. A loud botty burp came out then the smell of poo filled the car. Boy, it was really bad too! How could a little baby emit such loud noises and make such a stench? Yuck. Then it dawned on me, he was just like his dad! Although his dad never pooped his pants, well, not that I know of.

Eventually, after another tirade of grumbling by both parents, we pulled into a layby so I could change Shane's smelly nappy. At last, peace was restored and with Shane nestled cosily in my arms, sucking greedily on the teat of his bottle and emitting loud burps from time to time we continued on our way.

It was amazing to be away from the home, out in the world with my son, I wanted everyone to see him, to know he was mine, I felt so proud. However, deep inside sat a monster. A huge dark creature that was just waiting to gobble me up, drag me down into the depths of despair and I didn't know if I would ever be able to escape it.

We were so close, so very close and there hadn't been any more resentment voiced by either of my parents, just a few little digs I managed to ignore. Shane had fallen into a deep sleep and as I held him, I could feel his little heart beating next to mine. He was so warm, I loved him so much. When I felt this love, I shut it away quickly, I knew what was to come. The monster was stirring in me again, thrashing around the closer we got to the nursery.

It was such a lovely place, a large old rambling house near open fields, and I sensed that this house had wrapped its arms of safety around an awful lot of children down the years. The staff were really friendly and kind to me, they showed me compassion and explained the practicalities of the nursery and gave me a sheet of paper with visiting times on it. I looked at it in amazement. What? I could visit him. This wasn't a final goodbye! Tears were pricking my eyes and a tiny droplet escaped to be quickly brushed away. My father had noticed and his irritation was plain to see; he told me to stop that silly nonsense and get a move on.

Why do they keep telling me to get a move on, hurry up etc.? Don't they know I am trying to prolong the goodbyes, the parting? They have no idea, do they? Of the pain the agony of what was happening. My mother had only once shown me some compassion. Not long after they'd discovered I was pregnant; I'd gone to bed and had been dozing. I felt a warm kind hand stroke my forehead and a gentle voice said, "You poor thing." The next day, she denied she had ever spoken those words and was back to her icy self.

Mum just stood there while I said my goodbyes. I placed my son in the cot we were shown to in a large bright and airy nursery on the first floor, tucked him in and with a trembling voice told him I was so sorry but there was no other choice. What a cruel mum I am I thought.

I so wished someone had come along and jerked me from this woozy sleep I was slipping into, it all felt so unreal. As I moved, I felt bewildered and lightheaded, in fact, really weird. It seemed as if I had reached out and touched something or someone my hand would go right through: that there was no longer any solidity Where was that person who could have helped to bring back the other Marys that were now trailing outside of her?

There was not one person through all of this who stood by me and asked what I wanted, how I was feeling. Perhaps if there had been, I would have found the strength to fight, cause ructions and demanded I keep my baby. I wouldn't have even contemplated leaving him there for strangers to look after.

What would have happened if my parents had just abandoned us there?

Goodbye beautiful Shane, goodbye my precious one, goodbye, goodbye, goodbyeeeeee. I gave him one last glance to imprint him into my mind. One big inhalation of breath to drink in his smell hoping it would stay forever. One last touch of his little hand. A large tear fell on his little face and he looked up at me. Our eyes met and I could see he recognised me and a warm smile broke across his face. Gently wiping the tear from his pale skin, I looked into his eyes deeply and begged him to forgive me.

What do I do with my empty arms, my empty heart; what can possibly fill that void? Would I ever love again and have other children? How would that feel? I guess I would just have to wait and see.

As the car crunched along the gravelled drive turned the corner and joined the queue of cars on the road to home, I looked back and gazed longingly at the house, I suddenly remembered a favourite poem of mine by Longfellow which had always moved me. I could so relate it to this old majestic house.

### THE OPEN WINDOW

*The old house by the lindens*
*Stood silent in the shade,*
*And on the gravelled pathway*
*The light and shadow played.*
*I saw the nursery windows*
*Wide open to the air;*
*But the faces of the children,*
*They were no longer there.*
*The large Newfoundland house-dog*
*Was standing by the door;*
*He looked for his little playmates,*
*Who would return no more.*
*They walked not under the lindens,*
*They played not in the hall;*
*But shadow, and silence, and sadness,*
*were hanging over all.*
*The birds sang in the branches,*
*With sweet, familiar tone;*
*But the voices of the children*
*Will be heard in dreams alone!*

*And the boy that walked beside me*
*He could not understand*
*Why closer in mine, ah! Closer,*
*I pressed his warm, soft hand!*

– *Henry W Longfellow*

One day, the nursery window will be wide open in this grand house that was a nursery. There would be no more Shane, just an empty cot waiting for a little form to take his place. Where will my baby be? A ghostly shiver ran through me, time was running out.

I can't explain what the journey home was like, I know I sat muted in the back of the car tucked into the corner, my arms wrapped over my chest trying to comfort myself and not really succeeding. Mum had that brittle look on her face and her lips were clamped. Dad was just concentrating on driving or so I thought. Suddenly a harsh voice drew me out of my reverie.

"What's the matter with you?" Dad asked.

With a pitiful voice, I muttered, "Nothing."

Inside me, something else was playing out. Dad, you have no idea, have you? No comprehension of what I might be feeling. I could feel the tears welling up, I felt panic throughout my body too. I'm going to lose control I thought, just freak out like some madwoman. I can't cope with this I want my baby back!

Dad glanced in the mirror but couldn't see me huddling further down in the corner, thank goodness. With a total lack of understanding he started bleating, "Well, it's done now until he's adopted. If you hadn't been so stupid, we wouldn't all be going through this. Now put it out of your mind, I don't want to hear any more about it. Your mother and I have had enough of your messing, we thought you'd have had more sense."

No one really spoke much for the rest of the journey apart from a few bickering exchanges between the front seat occupants. Thirty miles seemed like a hundred to me, we seemed to be travelling for hours when in fact it took less than an hour. I felt so cold and everything seemed so far away, it was a strange feeling, as though I was suspended in time somewhere but didn't know where. It was like I was looking down on myself seeing the wretchedness of me. This girl, this young woman took on a new guise—'Automated Mary'.

The smell of Shane stayed with me for days. I didn't want to change my clothes afraid it would disappear, and of course, eventually, the smell dwindled away. Something else of him was gone, the void was getting bigger. How I wished during my restless nights, when dark hands seemed to want to claim me, take me to a dark, dank place that they would. I willed myself to die, holding my breath for as long as I could, thinking of different ways of ending everything, then realising I was too much of a coward to do it anyway.

I'm not much use at anything, am I? What a bad person I am for messing up my life and those of my parents too. Just think what they'd had to put up with, the neighbours gossiping, their sly looks and underhand digs; they'd all gotten to know somehow. I could just imagine my mum gossiping too. "You'll never believe what Mary's been and done, got herself in the family way, she's caused no end of trouble, but we've stuck by her, of course."

'Stuck by me'—what did she mean by that? Just imagine how hard it was to drag myself out of bed and go to work, to face the looks of the neighbours who then turned away sniggering. I felt so ashamed. What about my knight? Well, I'd never seen him since that fateful day at the House of Shame. I'd wanted to, but didn't, if that makes any sense. These things all played out in my head, a constant circle of recrimination, self-hatred and a death wish.

We hadn't been home long when Dad came and stood in front of me. "That's it then, I don't want to hear another word about it until some solution has been found. Your mother and I have had enough!" He turned slowly as though he had suddenly aged years and walked away rubbing his head, shoulders sagging and I stood there in silence. Why do they keep blaming me? It's so unfair.

The room seemed to go icy cold, the hairs prickled on the back of my neck. A memory of a pair of hands clasped tightly around my brother's neck as he lay on the floor flashed through my mind and disappeared as quickly as it had come. Shivering I gasped.

My dad had had a violent father who could easily pick up a wooden chair, smash it onto his leg and break it into pieces, but he never hit the kids. I guess that was some consolation. However, it had resulted in Dad carrying deep-seated anger and that was often let loose on me and my brother.

I wasn't brought up in a house of love and kindness, fear lurked everywhere. Yet Dad was a different person in his garden happily pottering, planting, tending this and that. As a young child, he encouraged me to help him; they were peaceful, happy times we shared. But his conflicting behaviour engendered in me confusion for sure in my little mind. These moments of happiness were tangled with fear that constantly lurked in me.

Oh, those who have silenced me in my short life, have you ever thought of what you did to me, of the effect on this girl? I think not! Of course, I obeyed. I had to be the good little girl and then, just then I might get loved. But hell, I've probably blown my chances of that now. I'm a soiled girl, dirty, tarnished goods or whatever you like to call me; I'd sinned in the eyes of so many. I cried myself to sleep hoping the shame I felt would be gone by morning: but it wasn't, it had made itself at home deep inside me and refused to leave.

# Chapter 8
## *Out of the Blue*

Time passed so slowly; it seemed endless. Things seemed to happen around me as the waiting began, the wait for the day he would no longer be mine, the day he would become someone else's. I began to switch my mind off to it all. I seemed to have done this in stages, gradually pushing it all into the distance keeping me safe from this living nightmare.

I gave myself a talking-to and began to socialise a little. Friends dragged me out, but I only went through the motions. One day I laughed and then fled home feeling so guilty that I had laughed when my baby son was in a nursery without his mum. I told myself I had only borrowed him for a short period of time. That some mysterious plan was at work, that I was meant to go through this to bring joy to someone who couldn't have a baby.

Life went on, automated Mary found a new job, settled in, and adjusted to life without a bump, without Phillip. My bus journey home gave me a chance to fantasise about how it could have been but always when the bus went over a bump, I was jolted out of my wasteless imaginings. Tired and listless I arrived home, turning the key in the door I heard my father calling out. "Come here, Mary, right now." I couldn't believe what I was hearing; out of the blue, he told me they would take me to see Shane in the nursery if I wanted to go. Want to go? Of course, I did, didn't I?

We went. However, I wasn't too sure if it was a good or bad thing but the longing won in the end. Mum and Dad were actually pleasantish on the day; no bickering which was most unusual. Perhaps they've had a change of heart after all, I hoped so. Wouldn't it be wonderful to hear them say, "Well, Mary, we've been thinking, we've decided that you can bring Shane home and we'll look after you both. You can go back to work and we'll ensure he's taken care of. We realise all this has been terrible for you and we just can't rob you of your son. After all, he is our grandchild."

I was brought back to reality when Dad told me in no uncertain tones that this visit didn't mean they had changed their minds. Dad raised his voice somewhat, "He has to be adopted, there are no two buts about it. Mum just thought a nice ride out would be good and we might as well call at the nursery, there's some nice scenery on the way."

\* \* \* \*

Shane had grown, he was so podgy, still very fair-skinned; pasty my mum called him. Much to my surprise, he didn't have a lot more hair than when I had last seen him a few months before. What he did have was blond and silky smooth; bum fluff my dad called it. He'd outgrown all the clothes I had left him with so he was dressed in one of the outfits the nursery provided. It wasn't to my taste but then I had no say in the matter. How happy I would have been to stroll with my son to the shops and buy some clothes then take him back to our place where his daddy was waiting. At least he seemed well and happy, his gurgling made me smile. The girls that looked after him told me he was such a good baby, that he loved his food and slept all night now. How sad I was missing all these things and soon I would be missing him forever. Is there no justice in this world? His dad didn't have to go through any of this. It felt like I was being tortured, how I hated him in that moment.

Bless you, my precious son. Have you missed me? Have you realised I wasn't around looking after you? Are you scared now Mummy's gone? Oh, my gawd, I am a mummy! I had never taken that in. A mother, a mum at sixteen. Jesus, that's me. A mummy to this little baby whom I abandoned in a strange place with strangers. Mums just don't abandon their babies, or do they?

He started smiling and gurgling at me and oh! the feeling of lifting him from the cot and cuddling him into me was the most amazing feeling in the whole world. I couldn't help it, the love poured out and I clutched him to me never wanting this moment to end, but I knew it would. It was like some unseen hand waiting to reach down and snatch this moment of happiness from my life and leave me in the depths of despair.

I looked down at his little face and he smiled I smiled back and felt immense joy. I longed to take him home, look after him, let him know I wanted him and loved him. But there was no choice. Where would I go? How would I cope?

Dad told me one day, months before Shane was born that I had been very lucky, that years ago, women even ended up in Lunatic Asylums. He remembered when the local asylum was closed near our home a lady in her eighties had to be found other accommodation, she had been incarcerated for a very long time. Why? She'd got pregnant, up the duff, in the family way, had a bun in the oven. What a terrible ordeal for that woman, how could society do that to someone? I bet the father just carried on with life as normal. At the end of the day, life isn't always fair.

Before I knew it, Dad said, "Come along now, it's time to go, we can't be hanging around here all day, I've got jobs to get done at home and your mother wants to go to bingo."

"Bingo," I mouthed. "Bingo!" But my voice had trailed off into nothingness.

"You have no idea have you, no comprehension of what I might be feeling?" I could feel the tears rising up, I could feel the panic cascading through my body too. I'd thought I was going to lose control, freak out like some mad woman, feelings I'd had before fought to get out. I can't cope with this I want my baby, don't make me leave him here…please…!

He glanced up in the mirror but I hung my head tight-lipped shaking with sadness and anger. Off he went again repeating the same old stuff he'd said earlier more or less word for word.

"Well, he's here until he's adopted. If you hadn't been so stupid, we wouldn't all be going through this. Now put it out of your mind, I don't want to hear any more about it. Your mother and I have had enough of your messing. We thought you'd have had more sense!"

Didn't they realise I wanted to be loved, to feel love and warmth, to know that someone wanted me, cared for me? I wonder what that would feel like, it would be so alien to me. They'd never shown me any of it! And as for that smelly farmer with his wooden leg; the least said about him the better!

# Chapter 9
## *A Solution*

"Oh Mary, can you ever forgive yourself for what you have done? For the pain and suffering you have caused?" rolled round and round in my head and more was to follow. You bad girl, you bad, bad girl. How could you be so stupid? You've brought so much shame on yourself and others; nasty Mary! There was a mixture of voices chattering in my head, blaming me, shaming me. Stop it, stop it, it isn't true! I slapped my head and gave myself a good shake, yelling at myself to pull myself together. You did the best you could; remember, others made choices for you, things were enforced on you. Don't let their taunts haunt you for the rest of your life. But they haunted me long enough until I wanted to bring an end to it all.

Pretending everything was alright wasn't easy, I put on a front smiling at people as though nothing had happened, that all was well. I'd gradually detached myself more and more from the whole experience, I began just going through the motions. I'd see a hand picking up a cup not taking in it was my hand. I knew what was to come, I didn't know when or how the final going would come about but one day it would. Shane would be gone forever.

I've often wondered how someone felt waiting to be executed. Were they able to totally detach themselves from the gruesome thing that was going to be done to them? I don't know, but surely there are some similarities. I was going to die in some way, and that process had already started. I began praying for a miracle, a stay of execution. Please, oh please, don't let this terrible thing happen.

I tried to get on with life and had been seeing friends. I even managed to get a new job, but I was so unsettled. A dark cloud hung over me and soon this cloud settled so heavily that I felt suffocated by it. The telephone rang one day and when I answered the familiar voice of my sister-in-law came down the line.

"Hello, Mary, it's Sally here, I wondered how things were going, how you're coping, I know it must be difficult for you."

I sighed. I hadn't heard from Sally in a while, although she was my sister-in-law. There wasn't a straightforward way of contacting each other as she lived a long way, away so communication had been very sparse. After a few pleasantries, she stopped talking and I heard her take a deep breath as though she was pondering over what to say next. I hoped she wasn't going to be another person to dump me unkindly, but then she had enquired in a pleasant way about how I was.

"Shane's still in the nursery from what I've been told," She went on.

"Have you all been discussing me behind my back?" My voice was small almost a whisper. "I don't like to think people are talking about me unkindly, gossiping about the situation I'm in. It's all too horrible to bear." I burst into tears releasing the tension I'd been holding onto.

"Oh, Mary don't get upset, I know it's a shitty situation you're in. There's been such little support for you through all of this. I know what your parents are like, they're so cold and uncaring."

"Sally, it's been a nightmare and the worst's yet to come. Poor Shane's stuck in that nursery, although he seems really happy there, he was gurgling and smiling when I last saw him. Maybe he's miserable when I'm not there, who knows what might be happening to him?"

Sally said, "It's such a worry I know, love, but I think I might have an answer to your problem."

"Really," I gasped. "What is it, what on earth have you come up with?"

At this stage my mind became like cotton wool. A solution? My head started to ache. But…t… Social Services are sorting all the adoption process out filtered through. I tried to interrupt her; however, she just carried on.

"Well, quite by chance," she said, "a friend told me of someone she knew who was childless and that her husband had agreed to adopt a young baby and that they were quite happy to do a private adoption. They desperately want a child and would happily give my baby a loving home."

Apparently, they lived in London and I was so pleased that he would be with a couple who obviously would provide well for him living in the capital. How fortunate he would be, I could never have provided such things. I knew something had to be done, he couldn't stay in the nursery forever. He needed affection, love, security and of course stability in his life.

What's going on? Here I am enthusing about all this when plans are already in-hand, or so I thought? Did she know something I didn't? I felt totally confused.

"Really," I repeated in a nervous, monotone voice. "I don't know what to make of it all."

"Listen, Mary. First of all, I want to say that I am well aware you've had and are still having a really hard time with all of this. The way your parents have treated you is so cruel, they haven't been thinking of you at all, only themselves. I've always felt that you and Philip could have made a go of it together, after all, he did ask you to marry him, but they wouldn't have that, would they? Neither would his parents. I know you would have had to wait sometime before you could marry but at least you would have been given a chance to make a go of it."

The kindness in her voice started the tears again. "Sally, you are the only person to care how I am feeling over all of this. Thank you so much," came my now snotty reply.

"Yes," Sally said. "I've made a few tentative enquiries for you and I did speak to this person. She sounded really nice and she's not worried that it was a difficult birth, she feels that something would have shown by now if anything was wrong. I hope you don't think I'm sticking my nose in. I so want to help you, Mary, there's no one else helping is there? Oh, and she rang me from a friend so no information will be available about where he goes. It has to be kept confidential; are you OK with that?"

At this stage I was completely lost. My mind seemed to take it all on-board, and go along with it. I felt I was being dragged into something that I shouldn't be, but couldn't stop it. It was like being taken over. I was so scared. Just like so many things that have happened in my life, I felt helpless, vulnerable and small.

"That's alright, Sally, he has to be cared for and no, there bloody well isn't anyone else supporting me is there? It's been just me, all alone, as it has always been since I was small. A little girl lost since I came into this world. What a horrible place to be, with nasty people who didn't love me, didn't care, abused, used and battered me. What is life all about, nothing but crap, crap and more crap!" My voice petered out and I flopped into a chair.

This solution was a double-edged sword. Of course, an answer had to be found, and one had. Yet that would mean that soon, really soon, Shane would be gone forever, I would never see him again. The reality of what was to be closed its mean, nasty arms around me eagerly.

Knowing they were an older couple living in London sounded good, a wealthy city full of prospects for him; I didn't think to ask any more. They sounded to be a caring couple and what a shame they hadn't been able to have a child. At least, I could go on and have more children at some stage. Well, I hoped so, life surely couldn't leave me childless. That would be a mighty blow. They must be comfortably off I thought, and told Sally, "Yes it was an ideal solution, he would be loved and cared for and where they lived spoke of wealth and security."

I pondered over which part of London they lived in, but of course, that had to be kept a secret. Here we go again, this secret thing is trailing me now. But yet, don't we all have secrets under wrap and key, locked away in closets, buried deep within us, kept within the family maybe creeping out at some stage in life or maybe never being spoken?

Of course, behind the scenes, all sorts of arrangements were being made. I didn't ever actually know who made the plans, who spoke to who, at the time. I never asked. But later I was to discover that secret meetings with Social Services were held at home with my parents, when I was at work. Mum and Dad were very keen to follow through with this adoption, and of course I felt pressurised. Mum mentioned many times about Shane's terrible birth and all the lumps and bruises he had suffered that my mind eventually absorbed all this and I assumed there was a problem with the adoption agency following through as planned. After all Shane had been put in the nursery when other babies hadn't been. It's strange what tricks the mind plays when you're drip-fed things. And why was my sister-in-law so keen about this London adoption? Had there been other secret meetings, conversations going on? After all I was always left out of things. My heart was beating rapidly and I started shaking. I was to realise that it was my mum and dad who wanted this adoption to be settled quickly. And guess who just went along with it – of course me! I'd gone into 'this isn't happening' mode. It felt as though I was on another planet, out somewhere in space, a weird feeling for sure.

One day, my mum told me that it was all sorted, that this person would pay the local authority solicitor's fees (Social Services had obviously continued being involved) and they would give me fifty pounds to help me get on my feet. But as soon as Shane had gone, I started feeling ashamed and angry that I took this money. It suddenly felt as though I had sold him. The solicitor asked me about it and, in truth, it had never been mentioned until after the decision to let them adopt him had been made. Thank goodness the solicitor helped me understand that.

So, Shane was to go to his new parents, all the arrangements had been made; it was done behind my back. Here were adults making decisions for me yet again. When would it ever end? She, my mother, just told me matter of factly, it was all sorted and there was no going back.

But what did my mother decide on? Jesus, how stupid of her to insist that I fetch him from the nursery and have him home for the night! That was so bloody cruel! But I went along with yet another decision made by the grown-ups. To be honest, in my mental state, I didn't have any fight in me, I wasn't able to process any decision-making. My mind felt like a dried-up prune, shrunken into itself only allowing me to manage day-to-day life.

So, we needed somewhere for him to sleep, milk, bottles and teats, all the paraphernalia a baby needed. Going to buy a second-hand carry-cot for him from a stranger's house seemed unreal, it was turquoise and he only just fitted. It so brought home how much he had grown, how much I had missed and how time had gone by. I will never forget that carry-cot, it is etched in my mind. And that little person who was tucked under soft blankets in it, my son, will never ever be forgotten.

Panic was welling up; I could hardly breathe. The emotion was so powerful and it was pushing up, but I slammed a 'cap' on it. No, be strong, it's better for Shane, he needs two kind, loving parents to care for and provide for him. What could this anxious, bad mum give him; nothing of course.

# Chapter 10
## *Gone, Really Gone*

I dreaded that final journey to collect him from the nursery, every twist and turn in the road represented how my stomach was feeling. It was drizzling and scudding clouds chased each other overhead. My body felt so tense and my heart beat so loud, it's a wonder my parents couldn't hear it, the blood seemed to pound in my ears. If the car had crashed on that journey and I'd been killed it would have been a relief, I would have escaped what was to come.

At last, the car was crunching along the drive, the large house looming before me. My legs shook as I got out of the car and trailed behind my parents into the house; we were expected. One of the nursery staff looked at me and a soft pair of hazel eyes made contact with mine, I could sense compassion, an unspoken understanding. My eyes welled up but one look from my father stopped the flow of tears in an instant.

I climbed the winding staircase wondering how many other mothers had made this journey and had known this was to be the parting from their little one. Stumbling across the nursery floor I breathed deeply and there he was in his cot. As I looked down at him, he turned his plump cheeks towards me and smiled, started to gurgle as before but also kicked his legs around in a little frenzy. The fight in me began. I can't do this, can't let him go, can't be without him, I'll never see him again! On and on my mind raced until I felt I would be sick.

My father's voice full of frustration rasped across the room, "Come on, Mary, get a move on, I can't stand around here all day. Your mother wants me to pull some rhubarb for her, you know I like those pies she makes with some of that lovely creamy custard. We've wasted so much time over this situation you got yourself into." Dad's voice held that terrible angry tone that I'd so often heard. I remembered how I had trembled as a child and tried to hide when he went off on one.

"Well, I don't care a shit about your bloody stupid pie and I hope the custards full of lumps," I snapped back.

"Now don't you talk to me in that tone, girl, you keep that mouth shut like you should have your legs. I'm going out to the car. You're so ungrateful, do you know, that ungrateful!"

With an immense weighty feeling in my stomach, I picked Shane up. The nursery assistants had already said their farewells and I thanked them for looking after him. With a bowed head and tears dripping onto the shawl I'd wrapped tightly around him, I walked from the room, down the staircase and out through the doorway, the heavy doors hanging menacingly aside me. Something stirred in my mind, where had I seen doors like this before? A shiver ran through me.

Dad stood by the car and scowled at me. For someone so small in stature, he was really scary just by the looks he gave at times. "Get in, will you?" He threw at me. "Stop messing about. I've told you already I need to get that rhubarb sorted for your mother. She's such a bloody nag!"

"Get a bloody move on, Mary, you heard what your father said," a screechy voice wailed. Now she was joining in. Stupid woman! Mum was clearly agitated as she was shuffling her feet and waving her arms around. I remember thinking I hope the bloody rhubarb chokes them! If I'd had a stick in my hand, I am sure I would have lost the plot and whacked them until they could experience pain like I was experiencing.

Eventually, we arrived home. The key turned in the lock and the front door creaked open, the chipped and mottled paint seemed even shabbier. As I walked into the hall and struggled up the stairs noticing the faded colours of the stair carpet and its ragged edges. I sighed deeply. I'd never noticed the stale smell of the place before, it seemed as if all my senses were enhanced.

The sleeping baby held safely in my arms had been so good on the way back, taken his feed well and only peed his nappy a little, although I could feel dampness seeping through the shawl now.

I shut myself in my bedroom and stared at the turquoise carry-cot, it looked alien beside the bed. Shane stirred and I carefully changed his bum, burped him some more and cuddled him as close to me as I could without hurting him. I clung on never wanting to let him go but knowing I'd have to.

My arms were wrapped lovingly around him. In that moment, I could feel love seeping from my broken heart. Of course, it had been there all the time but I had forbidden myself to really feel it, to let him feel it. I'd had to protect myself from what was to be. He was a little miracle, well not so little now. A miracle that Phillip and I had created. Looking back, I see the significance of two people being able to bring

74

new life into the world. I wished I'd known what was happening all those years ago, that I had been aware of what a 'special kiss' was! But why, oh why, had just one sperm been an Olympic swimmer so determined to reach its goal?

"Oh, darling baby, Mummy is trying to help you have a good life, that's why I've got to do this and sweetheart people have told me it has to be this way, I've no choice! After all, you deserve better than me, I am such a bad person." The word 'wicked' spun in my head, it was Mum's favourite word for me. "You wicked Child!" she'd yell. And mums knew, didn't they? They only spoke the truth, or so I thought.

A voice shouted up the stairs, "You'd better make sure you're up and ready by nine o'clock, your mother's got a long journey, she'll be worn out when she gets back so you had better have the tea ready my girl!"

I chose to ignore him, a mistake really.

"Are you listening?" and he shouted even louder and repeated what he'd said.

Muttering through trembling lips I replied, "Yes, I heard."

"Speak up, will you? You know I'm deaf."

"I bloody well heard you, why don't you put your stupid hearing aids in? Huh. I'd like to get a stick of that bloody rhubarb and stick it right up your arse!"

"What's that you said, girl?"

"Nothing, Dad," and I slumped on the bed in despair.

The night drew in, dark shadows filled the room. They were like ghostly figures moving around, I'm sure I was imagining it all, well I hoped I was. More trouble was to come as I wouldn't eat any tea. I got all the ungrateful stuff yet again. Let them get on with it I thought. Later in bed I tossed and turned but bless him, Shane only woke once. He loved his milk, sucking so loudly, burping even louder and filling his nappy with squishy sounds and making a stench I don't want to think about. My plan was to stay awake all night, to listen to every strange noise, every breath he took, but it didn't work.

A banging on the bedroom door woke me with a start.

"You up yet, Mary? You know what your father told you, I have to leave in an hour."

What? No, it can't be only an hour. Shane started crying, I started crying and we cried together, clinging onto each other, trying to get inside each other so we couldn't be parted. It was as if he knew what was going to happen. I knew well what was to come. Please, don't let this happen, this just can't happen, if there's a God out there stop this terrible thing. But these forlorn pleas fell on deaf ears. He was fed, burped, changed and dressed, wrapped in his now-dried shawl, a fluffy hat covering his fair hair. I'd packed a spare bottle of milk, some spare nappies and a change of clothes in case of accidents.

"Shane I… I…love you. Take that love with you, know that in the deepest recesses of your heart my wonderful son, I love you. Let that love go with you wherever you go, I hope it keeps you safe." But I knew I was only saying these words; my heart was on lockdown; I couldn't connect with the feelings and emotions. At least, I had whispered the words in his little ear. My ears pricked up as I heard the footsteps creak on the stairs, I waited and then a fist banged on the door and a screechy voice shouted.

"Give that baby to me now or I'll be late, get a move on."

There was only a distance of about eight paces to reach the bedroom door but I took the smallest steps I could, prolonging what was to happen. Just as my hand caught the doorknob, my father's voice boomed out.

"Get a move on, will you!"

Can't they think of something else to say other than 'Get a move on'? Stupid people!

I was on the landing now, facing my mother, her face drawn and an icy glare plastered on it. I could see wrinkles that were starting to appear and signs of grey in her hair. She's aged I thought and it's all my fault.

"Come on give him to me, stop messing about," and she jiggled her arms around enticing me into placing him there.

That's just what I did, I put him in those arms, gave him to that iceberg of a woman, a woman devoid of any feeling for me, her daughter, her own flesh and blood and what she was going through.

Time stood still, I felt encapsulated in space, nothing was real. She turned and walked away, a trail of scent from the baby powder I had used hanging in the air. I heard her footsteps on the stairs, I counted each one hearing the familiar creaks and groans. Then the rattling of the letter box as the front door opened. My dad's voice filtered up the stairs, his words inaudible to me. Then another familiar sound of the door knocker banging as the door slammed shut. I stood gasping for breath, fixed to the spot. I looked down at my arms, at the emptiness there now, where a few moments ago my son had lain, warm, secure and loved. The pain began in my chest; it was like sharpened knives piercing into my flesh. I screwed my eyes uptight hoping the tears wouldn't flow, but they did.

I suddenly picked up another sound that filtered through a fog in my mind. Footsteps trudging along a path, they were fading into the distance now, then all became quiet. I raced to the front bedroom and stared out the window. I froze as I saw my brother helping them into his car. What the hell! So he was party to this too. Waves of anger rose up in me, it was sharp and jagged. I trembled with the intensity of it.

I stumbled back into the bedroom shocked at what I had seen, sat on the edge of the bed looking at the turquoise carry-cot, the indentation of his body still visible in the bedding. Gone reverberated in my head gone!

Becoming aware of a presence in the room, I opened my eyes and looked at my dad. He stood there just staring at me, his small frame upright and an angry scathing look spread across his face. His staring continued and it unnerved me. Now I was twitching and it joined hands with the trembling. Then suddenly he shouted, I wrung my hands frightened he'd hit me but he didn't.

"You are never to speak of this again, never." And sighing he turned, walked away and left me frozen to the spot.

I was so good at doing what was demanded of me, so I kept my mouth shut! Not realising that doing this would lead to bouts of anxiety and depression that would trail me through life.

Gone! Gone! Reverberated around in my head as a clamp gripped my heart numbing my feelings.

What did I have left? I felt so empty. I was a living, breathing mass of bones and flesh. There was no anchor in my life to hold me steady. It was like I had been thrown in a sailing boat and allowed to flounder on a rough sea. Maybe those waves would wash me overboard and take me deep down in the sea and all would be over.

My nightly dreams of seeing my baby floating around in a vast ocean were difficult to deal with. Every time I reached out to take hold of him, he moved further away until he was way out in the distance a mere shadow. The dreams eventually stopped, after all, there was nothing left to take hold of.

# Chapter 11
## *I Can't Stand Anymore*

The years rolled on things happened, people came, people left but I never really settled and then one night! What the hell? A restless sleep, tossing and turning as though something inside of me churned around, an internal conflict was taking place. What was going on? I rolled out of bed stubbing my toe on the bedside table and flinched with pain. Clumsy bloody woman, I muttered.

I could feel it then, it was so tangible as though I could reach out and grasp it in my hands. From somewhere deep inside of me, a longing stretched like a piece of elastic into an invisible distance. What lay there in those places I knew not, or maybe I did but didn't want to venture there. Was it a journey I even wanted to embark on I asked myself?

I don't think I will rest until I have the truth, uncover the answers, dig deep into the unknown to discover and make known what happened to my son. Yes, my son. That tiny vulnerable baby I was forced to give away when I was only sixteen. My first-born!

I was sitting on the bed now and sensed a quiver running through me. The tension in my body intensified. How clever I was at being able to block my emotional pain in this way. I became aware my feet had lifted off the ground slightly caused by my pelvic girdle tensing so tightly; the constricted muscles had pulled up my legs. Relax, Mary, relax, you may be in your fifties now but it is never too late to find out.

But is it? What lay ahead, I mused. I was stepping into what I felt was a spinning vortex and that was really frightening for sure. Wasn't my life more settled now, didn't I have wonderful things happening especially with my counselling and healing work and the people I came into contact with through all of that? Oh, and my two beautiful children, a son and a daughter, so precious. No one will ever take them away from me, I would fight and fight to keep them.

Can you imagine what it's like to have your baby, yes, your baby taken from you by your own mother and whisked away to who knows where and given to complete strangers? And realising my own brother being party to it too. It's like having a part of your body ripped away like a tooth being pulled from its socket with no anaesthetic. Just imagine that pain...

As I stared out of the window, now steamy with my breath, I sensed the wind's grabbing fingers grasping at the trees. The strength of the wind pulling and tugging the branches haphazardly trying so hard to wrench them into pieces. Then letting go as the force abated allowing the trees to stand upright again like sentinels in the night, calm and still and then the wind restarting its ferocious attack.

Turmoil then peace, a reflection of myself. However, at this moment in time, as in so many other moments, the peace element was ever elusive.

Secrets, oh boy, secrets. As human beings, we carry them through life, sometimes even to the grave. A burden, a weight pressing us down, dancing around inside of us, an unspeakable and for some unmentionable. Locked away in our unconscious our sub-conscious, trapped in a bottomless pit but there nonetheless.

Rain unexpectedly lashed against the window, the sudden noise startled me and prickles spread over my skin as a cold wave of apprehension flowed through me. The night wrapped its arms around me and I fumbled for the light switch, knowing it would provide comfort by transforming the gloom into brightness. Where the bloody hell was it? I was rubbing my hand across the wall, up and down side to side. Come on, come on—blast you! At last, I located the switch and the sudden brightness that burst into the room made me screw my eyes up.

You can see how brave I had to be to even think about finding my son, it resurrected so much that I needed to deal with. But I know in the long run, it will be a healing journey for me. I will be setting myself free of what I have locked away inside. Dad! I won't keep my mouth shut anymore, I am opening it wide and speaking my story for all to hear.

How proud I am of myself to have come through this, like so many other poor women we've survived. At least society is acknowledging this subject now, realising there were amazing women in society, who, for one reason or another found themselves unmarried mothers. The words illegitimate or bastard were so readily used to describe babies born out of wedlock years ago, thank goodness that is no longer the case; well, possibly there are exceptions.

I was rubbing my tummy now remembering, allowing the past to draw me back, take me to those places of isolation, loneliness, sadness and pain. Slumping back onto my storm-tossed bed, I let the hands of time do their worst and they did it well.

# Chapter 12
## *Revelations*

Somehow, an opening appeared between the fog that was swirling in my mind, the opening became larger and gradually as clarity came, I could see something. Yes of course the file! Emblazoned on the front of it in large bold letters: **DAVID MY SON**. I had done some research years ago and discovered his name had been changed. However, back then I found tearing open the deep-seated wounds was too much to bear, and put everything away in the back of a cupboard. Then I remembered the other file I had too. **'Keep Important Documents'** births, marriage, divorce and death. None of the death stuff yet thankfully.

My mind was playing tricks. I could almost smell my baby, the fragrance of baby powder that I used to rub gently onto his soft pale skin became stronger, such a sweet reminder of his little self.

Are you crazy or what? I muttered out loud. My hand trembled as I picked up both the files, their edges tattered and torn. But there was a certificate inside this file that represented a death of sorts to me. My heart somersaulted. I dared, yes, I dared to pull this monumental piece of paper from inside the file, I dared myself to unfold it, I dared myself to read what was on it. Yes, I dared! The pain poured out. It felt like a surgeon's knife had run across my heart slicing deep, re-opening a wound that had never really healed.

My eyes stared wide at the birth certificate of my son, my beautiful Shane. I trembled and sat unceremoniously on the floor clutching the paper in a shaking hand. My mouth had gone dry and I was aware the shaking in my hand had now extended to the rest of my body. I felt dizzy and sick.

Darling Shane, where are you? I do so hope you are well my precious baby. Have you been happy? Is your life blessed with fun and laughter? Oh, my darling, I am daring to miss you in this moment, allowing myself to feel for you; feel the wounds left with me.

Philip's betrayal and my mother and father's cruelty still haunted me and it continues to trail behind me, like some huge metal-linked chain with an anchor on its end that is firmly hooked into the past.

My hatred for what my parents did, especially Mum still batters the door inside me to be set free, and it scares me. If I gave into its 'attention seeking' what would happen? Would I become totally deranged and end up sectioned in some mental institution never to be set free?

I felt so frightened, these feelings were so intense. How I hated it, how I wanted to scream at Social Services who told me it was for my own good that my baby should be adopted. Their words flew around my mind; I just wished they would fly away so I could forget. I felt badgered as they kept repeating, "You are too young to bring a child up, where would you live? Your parents won't have you at home. It's best for the baby. You're too immature, too this too that." Isn't that bullying, brainwashing?

For me, I just kept thinking what a rubbish person I was to have been such a bad girl. I'm just no bloody good. That's the crux of the matter, I'm not even good enough to keep my baby, be a mum.

Then my dad's words were ringing and clanging in my head until I grabbed my hair, pulling and yanking it until the roots burned and ached. You dirty disgusting thing. You slut! I could feel his foot kicking me, hurting me while a volume of abuse was hurled at me. But I didn't know what I had done to get pregnant. My mind remembered the words that screamed inside my mind. "Let me be dead, let me be free from this suffering." On and on, on and on he went, my dad, my father yelling at me. "You're not keeping this baby; do you hear me? I won't have you here, you're trash." With a look of utter disgust, these final words roared from his snarling lips. "You'll have to go into a home. You're not wanted here!"

I uncurled my aching body, eased myself from the floor and staggered up to my room. The word 'Home' echoed in my mind raced around gathering speed. Like a car taking part in some grand prix, it raced, tore round corners with such a force until the words 'Home' hit the finishing line and the little girl inside me quivered. No! Not the giant's castle again where nasty boys come in the dark and do nasty painful things to me no…ooohh! But that's another story…

Then a click in my head scared me and I was once more dealing with my mind relaying the scenes of a young vulnerable damaged child of fifteen being led up the stairs by a young man of eighteen, it was all so clear. The confusion of not knowing what was happening and then the discovery at work when Pat made me realise we had done '*IT*' and that I was going to have a baby.

The shock horrors came racing back with a force of an eighty-mile-an-hour gale. I reached out a hand and steadied myself, shifting my position so I was now supported by the wall. In a strange way, the wall felt comforting, it was solid and strong while I was weak and falling apart.

As scene after scene unfolded, I breathed deeply to prevent the panic from rising full force and taking me over. The parents arguing, Philip's proposal, their scathing remarks; casting aside what would have changed my life and provided the security for Shane, preventing the nightmare that was to unfold. I'd forgotten how bad, how terrible it had been. Gulping air in, I slid to the floor pushing hard against the wall pulling my legs up and hugging my knees tightly, so I felt some human contact.

The shame and the guilt poured in as I saw her walking up the steps and then through the door into the entrance hall of the unmarried mothers home. As I focused on this girl, large tears dropped ceaselessly down making a damp patch on my skirt.

She was in the hospital now. In a room, where strangers fiddled around inside her until copious amounts of fluid streamed from her body splashing onto the floor and then it began! The unbearable, excruciatingly razor-like pains that gripped her belly, ravaging her flesh, making her cry out in terror, "Stop! Please stop!" The theatre lights streaming down, her legs being forced into some indescribable metal stands. Pain racked her young body and then there was darkness and nothingness as the needle did its job and sent the liquid around her veins.

As the stitches between her legs tight and scratchy from the tears in her tender flesh pulled, I watched her walk, grimacing with pain, to the special care unit to see her son, pale and still with a lump and huge bruise on his forehead. His entrance into the world had been as hard for him as it was for his mother. Yes. That was me, his mother. The days and nights of tending him back in the unmarried mothers' home, of staring frozen and petrified at him knowing what was to come.

They were all there. The sequences of events unfolding and now the final one. The turquoise carry-cot before her so carefully supporting her baby while he slept. His little hand made into a fist pushed under his chin. His blond hair close to his scalp seemed to shimmer in the morning sunlight that streamed through the window. She lifted him gently while her mother looked at her cold and foreboding. "Come," she seemed to say, "that's it," the girl's mother continued. As she held her arms out, the girl in a dream-like state, as though someone else was moving, shifted and placed the baby into the outstretched arms and let go. The mother's arms curled around the sleeping babe. He slept on oblivious to what was happening, that the course of his life was changing in an unimaginable way.

The footsteps on the stairs and the front door crashing did nothing to awaken her from her trance. Then a stillness settled and the empty cot was before her. Her baby was gone, gone forever and ever—a living death had occurred.

Her father's voice rang out loud and clear, "You are never to mention this again." Then a door slammed shut in her head to it all.

The zombie girl turned, lying stiff and motionless on the bed. Pain so intense. But she was numb to it all. It felt like a thousand whips had lashed against her flesh and penetrated her young heart. No tears just the thoughts roaming her mind. The silent screams racked her body. **I hate you all for forcing me into this!**

The scenes faded and I forced myself to sit at the table pen poised. As the ink transferred onto the paper the words became clear. Dear Mrs Thompson…

Yes, I discovered that this was the lady who had adopted Shane and I am writing to the address on the adoption certificate. I have nothing to lose but I might have something so wonderful to gain.

Not an easy letter to write. What do you say to an adoptee's mother? How do you explain the need to know, the longing for information about your own son, someone she had brought up, raised as her own?

As I penned the address onto the envelope, my hand weaved around. It looked more like the scrawl of an eighty-year-old than a fifty-something. I slipped a stamped addressed envelope alongside the letter and as I sealed the flap, I prayed they still lived at this address. It was a long way down the line now, but you never know, they just might still be there.

Strolling up to the post-box alone, a sad-faced dog left behind, I felt like I was that sixteen-year-old Mary. I fumbled with the letter as the gaping mouth of the bright red post-box stared back at me. No. I can't do this, it's too much to bear and the envelope dropped to the ground.

"Ups-a-daisy," a young voice said.

Turning, a lad of about nine stood looking at me, his eyes filled with the excitement of life. "I'll get it," he mumbled.

Grubby fingers clawed the envelope from the tarmac close to a pile of dried dogs' poop, and before I knew it the letter was thrust eagerly into the void, eaten hungrily by the postbox's gaping mouth.

"There you are, lady, all sorted," and he skipped off whistling loudly a proud grin on his young face.

Jeez, shit, hell's bells and buckets of blood, and I just stared boggle-eyed. What the bloody hell had I done or that stupid boy done? Turning I plodded home and wrestled open a tinny, gulping down the chilled liquid eagerly.

# Chapter 13
## *Postie, I Love You*

Months later, I was staring out the window resigned to the fact I wouldn't hear from Mrs Thompson, perhaps I was being impatient, who could blame me? When you long for something so much it's natural to want answers really quickly.

I'd opened the window to let some fresh air in and my attention was caught by the sound of whistling followed by the footfall of the postman who turned down my front path. My heart leapt. I didn't recognise the tune but I stared hard at the post held tightly in his manly hand. The letterbox clattered and I stood stock still; I expected it to be another bill.

Post? Images flashed into my mind of a red post-box, a young lad bright and perky full of the innocence of a child. Of him scooping a letter off the pavement, of the dried dog's turd settled on the tarmac close by. The young hand dropping the letter into the wide smiley mouth of the post-box. Letter? Letter? Oh, my gawd, the letter to my adopted son's mum. That was some months ago, and I'd heard nothing. "See, Trixie, that was a waste of time, wasn't it?" She wagged her tail as if agreeing with me. What an amazing faithful dog she was too: I so loved her.

My brain seemed to have a natural regressive action as I saw my hand penning the letter and as I watched the address and contact number settle on the page, I trembled. It was my old address, my disconnected phone number. How could I possibly receive a reply? You stupid woman, do you not have any sense?

Admonishing myself for being utterly useless, I grabbed paper, pen and envelope and set to work. I didn't need the innocence of a young boy to post it, I would do it myself. Later as I walked Trixie round the block, I stood feeling proud and satisfied as the letter plopped down into the bottom of the post-box.

* * * *

The telephone was ringing and just as I reached it, it stopped. Blast. Who was that I thought picking up the paintbrush in my well-paint-splattered hand. I dipped the brush into the pot starting on the skirting board once more. Freshness was beaming out from the newly coated walls, and once the skirtings were done the room was complete.

Drat! Another hair stuck to the paint. Long nails were really helpful, they picked the offending blighters off very nicely, with a bit of scratching about.

The phone started up again and I dropped the brush down onto the newspaper. After all, I am a bit of a cheapskate to buy a proper dust cover... I rushed into the kitchen and grabbed the handset. Breathless I muttered hello down the line. A female voice spoke, one I didn't recognise. "Mary? Mary...?"

"Yes, that's me," I replied lolling against the worktop.

There was silence; it seemed to just hang there and then the unknown person spoke, "I'm David's mum, you wrote to me."

The first letter arrived some weeks later; it was a well-filled envelope and I clasped it eagerly between my hands. Joy and anticipation rippled through me. What had she said? Was there a description, a picture? Was I going to get a glimpse into my precious son's life? To get to this day had been a long tedious, painful journey, but now here in this white envelope lay what could only be a glimpse of heaven. However, I couldn't do it, not now, not until it was darker when I could shut myself in away from the world. Later as the light faded and clouds clambered together bringing darkness quickly, I gently slit the envelope open and carefully removed the folded paper. The envelope fluttered to the floor as I flopped onto the settee with nervous anticipation. "Come on Trixie, cuddle up, I need some morale support." She cocked her ears, wagged her tail and leapt alongside me placing her head on my lap.

The paper rustled as I unfolded the pages, and shaking I retrieved the photos that had tumbled onto my lap. My mind found it hard to take in the blond-haired toddler that stared back at me, and what a beautiful smiley face he had. This, this was my son, the baby who had so cruelly been taken from me. He was just…t…well lovely.

Pictures of him in his twenties lay clasped in a now sweaty hand. His hair was so like his dad's; blond, brown and tightly waved. His eyes were blue, transparent and hypnotic. I found it hard to connect with this young man. Who was he? A stranger, an unknown and that disappointed me. I hadn't expected to feel so detached from this older version who was my first-born.

The picture of the toddler drew me though, I could relate to him, a little vulnerable baby. My precious son.

I stared hard, my mind chasing back down the years until I was sat in the dead of night, bottle in hand watching puckered greedy lips work at the teat, sucking precious milk into his little body. A life-giving substance that had ensured his well-being and growth. The loud burps that followed as I gently rubbed his back, his head bobbing around and tiny legs draped over my pyjama-clad legs made me smile.

St Catherine's, the mother and baby home, the place where not only babies cried but the mothers too as they were separated from their little ones. It was a place of heartache, of tension. You could feel it build as the days grew nearer to another adoption happening.

I can't really describe the atmosphere, the experience. There aren't words to do it justice, or a way of putting the words together to express the experience fully.

Drawing my eyes back to the picture of David, a large salt tear fell, then another, and another and I hadn't even read the letter yet.

My eyes scanned the penned information. When he cut his first tooth, took his first steps, grazed his knee, started school etc. etc. It went on and on. She sounded kindly and so proud of her son. No! My son!

All of a sudden, the heat rose and flamed in my cheeks, I was so angry. I resented every moment she'd had with him. Who was she to write about these special times, precious moments with my son? Yes, my son!

It was cruel, oh so cruel and I couldn't bear it. The sluice gates flew open and the emotion flooded out, overwhelming me. Life just wasn't fair!

I'd known when I embarked on this search, that I was being brave. That all sorts of feelings and emotions would rise to the surface but I hadn't reckoned on anger!

The yearning for my baby was so intense, so powerful. I shook with the strength of it all. Just to hold him again, feed him, rock him, sing to him, play with him, even change his shitty nappies. But it was futile. What was the point? It wouldn't bring him back.

I rose, Trixie scrabbling onto the floor, startled by my sudden movement. "This is too much to bear, too hard, too painful, pet." She seemed to understand, glassy eyes stared back at me and her tail drooped between her legs. It was a solemn moment for us both. I grabbed the letters and pictures and shoved them into the back of a cluttered drawer. Out of sight out of mind so the saying goes.

Standing in the back garden, I let the cold night air weave its cool tendrils around me. Looking up a multitude of stars sparkled, twinkled in the dark sky. Heaven, was there really a heaven and were there really angels? They'd told us on our healing course if we saw a white feather it was saying an angel was near. There's so much of my story untold here, of life before and after this happening.

There was no white feather, no angel either. But a huge void of space that reached out to who knows where. There would always be that void in me too, left from the loss of my baby, I felt tiny, so vulnerable. What a cruel world I lived in— none of it made any sense.

All those years lost, which could never be reclaimed, recaptured. I'd been robbed of my son and I suffered so and still suffer. All those years of having panic attacks, being doped to the hilt, not being able to step out my door, a prisoner in my own home, a mess, a well and truly messed up person. But she, this Mrs Thompson had had him and that was so unfair. Have a pill, swig a beer, or a cake or two. Get some sleep, escape, close down, bang it up tight in your head, forget it ever happened. Now I was having to face it all and hopefully, a good ending will be mine at last. I do hope so!

Months followed of exchanging letters and at least I was able to tell my story of how I was given no choice and my mother had just taken him from me. Hers contained snippets of the family, what David had been doing in his life, his school days and the death of his first-born son. How very sad that he had suffered this loss.

I came to respect this lady, after all, none of it was her fault. She had provided a safe, loving home for David and that was important.

It felt a deep injustice, and I so wish I had had the maturity and strength to have fought to keep him.

The day a letter arrived from her saying David—it's still strange to have him called by a different name—had no wish to be in contact with me, that his life was fine as it was, I just knew at that moment that I couldn't go on corresponding. She went on to say that he was sat by her side as she wrote to me, that he knew about the correspondence but didn't want to read any of my letters. All hope had been dashed of us being reunited and I couldn't deal with it. Enough was enough.

That whole experience of communicating with Barbara had been a double-edged sword. It had helped provide a link to my son and the photos she sent of his toddler years and early teens gave me glimpses of who he was growing into. However, when she wrote and told me 'Shane' (why should I call him David?) didn't want to be in contact with me the pain of loss was resurrected all over again, it was just too much to bear. He was so close, so near but so very far away too.

Although her letters had been kindly and she seemed to really care about how traumatic it had been for me, it was only adding more anxiety and pain to the situation. What had been revolutionary was the truth came out about the lie my mother had told her, that I hadn't wanted to keep him. How my own mother could tell a blatant lie was beyond me, but then why be so surprised when my mother had treated me with such icy coldness since birth? What was nice was that Barbara told me she would never have adopted David if she'd known that I had been made to give him up; she thought it incredulous that my mother could take him from me in the way she did.

My father's words 'Never mention this again'! had damaged me beyond belief. The anxiety and depression, I had suffered, and the need for psychiatric treatment added to the pile of baggage already collected since my birth. I was even given electric shock treatment which terrified me and resulted in major panic attacks and strong medication.

Now those words don't hold such sway and talking things over with a close friend I realised I couldn't keep up the contact anymore. I wrote and explained that knowing he didn't want to be in contact had hurt me deeply and I needed to step back.

So, you see things never are as straightforward as you think they will be, and the fantasies we build in our minds don't always become real. The past had stepped into the present and I had no option but to deal once more with an unfulfilled fantasy and cope with the disappointment and push the whole experience into the background once more.

# Chapter 14
## *A Reflective Time*

Time moved on once more. I'd settled into life but again the past rose up and grabbed hold of me and wouldn't let go. So what choice was there, I had a choice, no one else could interfere, or tell me what to do. Something kept gnawing at me and the more I fought it the bigger the gnawing grew, so I decided to renew my search for 'Shane'.

I know I've written something of this story before. Through my training as a counsellor and life itself, I came to realise that we deal with things in layers. The enormity of a situation isn't felt in its entirety at the time. The brain has a way of protecting us, holding back some of the feelings, thoughts and emotions through trauma. Now for me, I see and feel it all so clearly as I write. I have no illusion, no detachment to the experience, it is very real. That is good because I know each time, I revisit some of my journey I will feel lighter and freer.

I'd been on a traumatic journey, and having found my knight in shining armour, I saw everything through rose-tinted spectacles. But I wasn't seeing the whole picture. The relief of having a boyfriend and hopefully being able to fulfil my parent's continuous statements: no need to do this, that or the other as you'll only get married drove me on. This was the one, he would solve everything. Little was I to know he would destroy so much in my life and create so much heartbreak.

So, a 'special kiss' that I later learnt to be 'sex' led to a baby growing inside me. I can never put into words the disbelief, the fact that my knight had taken advantage of me in this way and new life had started to form. I learnt some time later on, that when the sperm wriggles into the egg a spark of light is emitted. How amazing is that! I was a vulnerable fifteen-year-old. Later I came to understand that we didn't have 'full' sex but that sperm can survive outside the vagina and find their way to their goal. All I can say is they must have been lively little buggers!

The horrors of all this had left their scars; from parents arguing, demanding this and that, making choices for me, telling me how it had to be! I'd felt bemused, broken and stuck in the middle of a nightmare. Happiness had been short-lived, I'd glimpsed beauty, love, warmth. But then came hell which continued for a very long time. Darkness had tried to gobble me up then a light had shone around me but there followed nothingness; no feelings or emotions, just a void.

The unmarried mothers home had been a cold, dark place devoid of loving kindness and compassion; just like my parents' home strangely. You just had to get on and survive, live with what was to come, try and blank it out, hide it somewhere in the recesses of your mind. But I can assure you it snuck out and snapped at you at times. Like a crocodile swimming towards you, its teeth barred waiting to open its jaws wide and those sharp white pointy teeth snap onto you hard and fast. And every time these feelings came, they were stronger, stronger than me; it so tried to break me, wear me down.

Eventually, in the maternity hospital, I had experienced the horror of horrors. No one had prepared me for the giving birth thing. There was not one person that had talked to me, comforted me and explained what was going to happen. The pain was like thousands of red-hot knives searing through my young body. I shuddered as I remembered when I had been wheeled off into an operating theatre with lights. There was machinery, trolleys, people milling around wearing masks, strange noises coming from different directions. I was terrified! Those glassy eyes peering over masked-up faces could have been the eyes of anyone. They were alien to me, unknowns, strangers. Things were jabbed into my arm and then this floating hand came nearer and nearer until it forced a mask over my face and a strange, muffled voice kept saying, breathe, take long deep breaths. The fear had encapsulated me with a tightness coiling around me like an anaconda forcing life out of me. What's happening…?

I had never known such pain between my legs, any movement had brought tears to my eyes as it raced from the front to the back of my lower extremes, you know 'down there'!

My first sight had been of Shane in a special nursery lying in a plastic crib. He was so big and his head had already begun to show bruising and a large lump was starting to stand out from his tender skin.

Then she appeared—my mother—how I wanted her to disappear, to get from my sight. She started to blubber and got all the attention from the nurses, I just stood there, alone, bewildered, drugged, in pain, and wanting support and kindness. But she got the attention, didn't she? Trust her to turn on the taps, she'd always been great at manipulating people. I nearly shouted what about me? But what would be the point?

Eventually, back at the 'home', I struggled with everything. My light duties were scrubbing the stairs down into the basement and the stone-flagged floors. Every stretch of my arm, even the slightest movement of my legs caused excruciating pain in that tender place where Shane had been forced from me with forceps tight around his poor head.

Night-times had been unbearable, although there were several of us in a room, their babies seemed to sleep on and on. Sat in the dead of night I'd winded him, but moving to settle him more comfortably in my arms was crucifying. Salty tears had run down my face; I'd try to lick them away before they reached my mouth but failed miserably. I looked a miserable form, still shocked from the traumatic birth, with a future where the cruel hand of fate would fall hard. For the first week, I'd dragged myself around frightened the pain would tear at me, but gradually it improved and at least I could walk more normally. But oh, my tits were heavy and full, sore with milk—I'd bottle fed—but soon the pills worked and they shrivelled to their usual banana-shaped form. I remember talking to them when I was in my early teens trying to make them grow. Well, people talked to plants to make them grow and it worked. But my tits obviously weren't listening!

The visit from Shane's father was so bittersweet, I hadn't known he was coming; he just appeared. His whole attitude was unkind, I never understood why he'd turned up, what good did it do? Not wanting to see his son was unbelievable! It only caused more pain for me, more of the hurt stuff. I remember his surname was 'Sly' so maybe he'd lived up to that? However, he did, I learnt later, pay something towards my keep at the home. Sending him away because he wouldn't even look at his son, had been an angry reaction to the hurt I'd felt over that. There hadn't been any offer of support from him so I just had to get on with it on my own. Well, that's nothing new I remember thinking.

Shane was to have an unsettled life, it wasn't a very secure start for him, but that was how it had to be. He wasn't badly treated in the nursery; he seemed happy enough when I visited. But it is not the same as being given a secure loving home with parents in a stable relationship who nurtured and lived with him. I did the best I could as an immature sixteen-year-old who'd had no support, who felt totally lost amid the chaos of a heart-breaking situation.

I was so numb with all this that suicide never entered my head, but it did many times in later life as I tried to escape the memories and the loss of my son. Maybe if my own mother hadn't taken him from me, wriggled those arms out for me to place him in them it would have been a little easier.

To this day, I don't know how I came to a place of forgiveness for what she did, it took a long time, many meetings and discussions and although I never got the answers I wanted, it helped me having voiced my feelings. Sometimes with anger, sometimes with tears. In the end, nothing would change what happened and I had to find peace within myself somehow to live a happier life.

# Chapter 15
## *Finding My Way*

You may have wondered how on earth I have managed to navigate my way through all of this: at times I wondered myself. But somehow I have survived.

I felt I have been directed from a higher source, especially from the Angelic Realms who appeared in my life when I set up my counselling practice. Developing my gifts as a healer coincided with opening up as a clairvoyant and psychic. I wasn't keen on this but had no choice but to go with-the-flow so to speak. It was an amazing time of my life and a new Mary emerged yet again.

These gifts added a new dimension to my therapeutic work. I could see and sense things about clients that helped them understand why they were stuck in life. Professional counsellors receive lots of support through their supervisory sessions with a fully trained professional supervisor and of course personal therapy. I've had lots of that and it certainly was an amazing experience.

This journey with my son has been rather 'snaky' so many twist and turns, unexpected ones too.

My love of dancing has been something that lifted me out of the darker times for sure. Twirling and whirling set me free in some way, it certainly helped.

I became a walker. Planning and completing different routes, like the Severn Way and the Wye river walk took me into a deep connection with nature. I loved being on my own, finding my way along the trails; dealing with unexpected challenges which helped me grow and another part of Mary was found.

On a spiritual level, I began having an awareness I was being guided through dreams and ended up traveling to India and staying in various Ashrams and experiencing peculiar other-worldly happenings. I remember waking up one night and there were three old ladies standing by my bed, looking down on me. They were talking to each other quietly and I remember these words. 'We'll look after her.' They smiled lovingly at me, then each other. The scene gently faded away. I felt totally loved and at peace. The ten years I spent in Sai Ba Ba's Ashram at Puttaparthi changed me and I felt as if my heart was opening up to a blissful love each time I went. It was a challenging time too; all sorts of things happened and so much emotion rose up and bit-me-on-the-bum so to speak. I was on a mission to heal myself on a deeper level. I even glimpsed moments of joy and happiness. It's always been there deep inside me as it is for everyone. To find it is a joy.

Each Ashram I visited gave me the opportunity to learn more about myself, to let go of the suffering and heal. I began to feel that all of what happened to me in my life has given me a greater understanding of suffering and a deep compassion for humanity and their struggles.

In my work, Angels started showing me processes to use to help people heal the specific wounded parts they were carrying around. I feel so blessed to be able to help in this way. And blessed to continue on my journey to seek my son and have a happy relationship with him and his children.

And so my journey continues.

# Chapter 16
## *A Woman with a Mission*

So much time has passed, so many things have happened, lots of happiness mixed with sadness has brought me to this place. I've been blessed with the joy of marriage and two beautiful children. But my life had been tinged by mental health issues, some serious at times needing a lot of intervention; all that is another story though.

So, what's led me to embark on what I plan to undertake? It's almost as if some unknown being planted thoughts in my mind and just won't leave me alone. I feel I'm being gently nudged to take action. This is a journey with no prescribed outcome. It's a risk, it could be wonderful or heart-breaking, but I am prepared to take it.

Well, the decision has finally been made; I've found the courage now I'm nearly sixty to find my son, to slot some of the pieces together. It's like a jigsaw with some of the parts missing and I want to complete the picture, at least as best as I can.

I've dabbled a bit, you see; done a bit of research and then left it, until I felt brave enough to find out a bit more. I remember sending a letter to the address where I had last communicated with David's mum. I'd stood by the post-box hearing it plop into the darkness after a young boy had retrieved it from the ground and posted it for me. This time I wasn't wishing I could retrieve it as I did when initially writing to his adoptees. No, I was willing this one on its way, to bring me good news. A copy of the old one is by my side as I pen a second and I can't believe that it's been ten years since I sent that first letter. Alas, my letter was returned with a short note:

*Sorry, my son opened the letter by accident. I think David died two years ago; I am the new tenant, the council told me that the previous tenants passed on.*

Initially, when I read *David died two years ago*, my stomach somersaulted. It was as if my intestines had started a tango and became entangled in tight knots. Bile came up into my mouth and I started to retch; I could feel heat flushing my cheeks. I shouted, my voice raspy, there seemed to be tight invisible hands around my throat. Pacing up and down the room the note clutched in a sweaty palm I carried on, my voice now more of a howl, like an animal in a cold steel trap, its jagged teeth cutting into its bone and flesh. "Too late, it's too late he's dead!"

That's it! I knew it, it's always the same; things just never work out for me. Of course, I'm such a bad, wicked person. My mum had told me often enough. Hadn't she threatened to put me in a home and had done just that? I was just three years old. Of course I'm not loveable, I'm just bad, so bad I want to die.

Stop! Will you, this is old stuff! You are not to get caught up in this anymore, your ego is just tricking you. How easy it is for us to slip back into these old emotional patterns. The old merry-go-round of despondency and despair had crept in, life was just too hard. Often I've sat by my local river watching the swirling waters, trying to find the courage to throw myself in, to end it all. Right now, thank goodness, I recognised I was being irrational and pulled myself up short, calmed myself down and re-affirmed I was good, kind, loveable and worthy of finding my son, it's just a blip.

Have you ever had a feeling creep over you as though an unseen hand is trying to steady you? Calm you down? Well, that's what happened. I knew I had to re-read the note slowly, then go through it again, to digest what it was saying. The realisation dawned slowly like a soft, warm blanket was wrapping around me. *The previous tenants passed on.* On the second reading, I breathed a deep sigh of relief that gently escaped from my gaping mouth.

It wasn't my son David (I'm still trying to adjust to his new name) who was dead, it must be his parents! *That will teach you, Mary*, I thought, *you should have read it properly in the first place, not panicked.* I'd put myself through all this crap for nothing. He wasn't dead! It must be an excruciating experience to find out that a child you are searching for, or someone looking for their birth mother or father discover they are no longer alive. The emotions that they must go through just don't bear thinking about. Thank God, my David is alive, well hopefully alive as I didn't have that final proof yet.

This is the letter I wrote to my son.

*You may be surprised to hear from me but I have wanted to write to you for some time. I guess I have been a little hesitant in writing a letter being unsure of how it might be received, but now I feel more confident, so hence this letter.*

*So many years have passed since I was corresponding with your mum. It was lovely to know she understood how hard it was for me; she came across as a kind, caring person. I couldn't have wished for someone nicer to take care of you. I do so hope that you received the tape recording I made for you and that you were able to listen to it. I think about you often and wanted to keep the communication channel open just in case there was the possibility that you may be ready to contact me now. There is so much I don't know of your life and it would be wonderful to hear how life's been for you. The photographs your mum sent to me were lovely and I treasure them.*

*In December, I will be sixty and cannot believe where all the years have gone. I am happy in my work as a holistic therapist; I'm very passionate about it. Another pastime I enjoy is travelling. For someone who would never get on aeroplanes in her teens, I have ended up travelling the world. Your half-brother and sister are in good health as are their children. I do so hope that you are well and happy and that your mum and dad are too. Your mum did tell me that you were a driving instructor and I hope you are still enjoying your work. It would be lovely to hear from you, David, and learn more about your family. Take care of yourself and please remember you are loved and always have been.*

*Warm wishes,*
*Mum.*

The year was 2007 when I penned this letter and it took some while before I plucked up the courage to search the death registers and know that his parents had passed away for sure. It felt as if I had hit a brick wall and somehow, I had to circumnavigate it. I didn't have the strength to crash through it or jump over it so I let time elapse before I felt stronger. The 'what ifs' that crept in seemed to revolve around in my mind, tripping me up, making me feel down. I am my own worst enemy at times and tried hard to take control of my negative thinking.

Thank goodness for computers and search engines. I'm not a lover of technology myself but I managed with some determination to find how to research the appropriate registers. Having an address helped and of course, I'd known David's mother's name.

I discovered that his father Joseph, known as Joe for short I was later to learn, had died in December 2004, and that his mother Barbara had died earlier the same year in May. Gosh, both of them gone so close together, that's not easy to deal with! Then a revelation filtered through; my son was an orphan; both his parents were dead. Wow! Then a realisation dawned. He is not an orphan, is he? Because here I am, his real mum and she is well and truly alive!

So, my dossier of searches had grown having ordered and received copies of their death certificates.

Further investigations led to me checking for David's marriage certificate. Barbara had told me he had married and this may bring to light more information of where he might be. Ha Ha! I am getting good at finding my way around search engines and now in front of me is a marriage certificate for the year 1988 and on it was the address of his wife. Hooray, I could write to that address, I so hope she is receptive to my enquiries.

Perhaps I had been a detective in another life, I know in my work as a counsellor I felt like one. I called myself Miss Marples sometimes, as I was always looking for clues, links, etc. to help unravel client's life stories. All sorts of things were discovered in this process and I have just remembered something else; my son's mother told me in one of her letters. I'm having to steady myself here to share what I learnt. It was that David's first-born died as a baby. It's incredible that both me and my son know what it is like to lose a child. Rightly or wrongly, I used to think it would have been better if my son hadn't lived. You may think this a terrible thing to have thought, but the torture of living for years and years knowing he was alive but with someone else just cannot be put into words. Death would have been final, no one else would have had him; he would have just been mine for a short time, precious weeks maybe months. That isn't the way it happened though. So, I have had to live with it day and sometimes night, like clawing fingers clinging onto my shoulder. Thoughts would come sneaking up on me, battering their way into my mind when I was trying hard to forget, to banish the memories from my life.

My Shane, that's what I called him, my boy, my son, what right did anyone else have to get him? None! But it's done! This is how it is and there is hope that I will find him at last and maybe he will be more open to being in touch now his parents are deceased. *Perhaps I will never find him*, floated sneakily into my mind.

*Get up off the floor, Mary, be more positive. You are sinking down onto the ground, falling into despair again. I can feel the tendrils of 'what's the point' wrapping around my ankles, trying to trip me up. Be gone you! I must continue this search. It is now or never!*

I've mentioned before that I corresponded with Barbara, the woman who adopted him. Unfortunately, I discarded all the letters she'd written to me. The one that had arrived clearly spelling out that he didn't want to be in touch with me was the catalyst for withdrawing from this link. What else might I hear? I just couldn't bear the thought of things my son said being relayed to me in another letter.

It's strange now I look back, I really wished I'd kept them all, but I hadn't. But I did keep the pictures she'd kindly sent me, they are the most important link to my son, a snapshot of him growing up and a glimpse of the people who were party to that. Bless. My heart quivered with love as I gazed at those photos of him when they arrived and I drank him deeply into the very core of my being, they are here by me as I type— where are you, my precious son? But no voice answered me, no angel wings wrapped around me to comfort me or guide me. Yet again, I felt so terribly alone with all of this.

And then a realisation dawned, it was my baby I so wanted to find, to hold, to cuddle, kiss and smell. But that wasn't possible, was it? He's not a baby anymore; he's a grown man. I didn't want a grown man; I wanted my baby! I groaned and burst into tears. This is so painful, so heart-breaking, my baby doesn't exist anymore, I so wanted him to have been encapsulated in a time warp. Well, that's just such a ludicrous idea to have.

As a therapist of many years, I had to find a way to move on from seeing Shane as a little baby now, so this is what I did. I helped my Shane grow up, using visualisation techniques, something I use a lot in my work. Every day, in my mind's eye, I grew him. The pictures I had helped a bit, but I had so few of them. It was strange, but I had to change my idea of what I was looking for. Baby Shane was no more, he no longer existed! The little one I had gently lifted from the turquoise carry-cot and placed in my mother's arms to be taken away was no more. I had been craving and longing for an illusion of what had once been. He's Shane no longer, he's now called David a grown man in his late forties. Huh, he's still Shane to me and always will be!

The months rolled by and gradually, I was able to formulate in my mind, a toddler, a young boy going to school, going to work until he was an unknown entity, a stranger, a silhouette of a grown man. After all the years of therapy and trying to put it all into some sense of perspective, I realise I haven't done so well. Here right now I understand that I still haven't moved on from what I really wanted, and that was my beautiful baby son. Will this grief ever go away, disappear, stop gnawing at me, cease stamping around in me like elephantine-sized feet? I do hope so.

A friend suggested another source for searching, Facebook. Why had I never thought of that? After spending hours trawling through every possible permutation with the information I had, I gave up. I spoke out loud to myself, "No, girl! Do not get despondent, all will be well in the end." Will it or won't it, I pondered?

My daughter who had been such a wonderful support through all of this mentioned something one day that I hadn't considered. That was to search for any adoption agencies that specialised in re-uniting babies with their birth mothers. Initially, I wondered how much it would cost but then weighed up in my mind the cost to myself of not doing this. The decision was made; I was clear about the next step; I needed help with this; I had to find Shane.

# Chapter 17
## *The Search Goes On*

Norcap was discovered and I embarked on a course of telephone conversations, form filling and a lot of waiting. I came to understand I wasn't the patient person I thought I was, in fact, I was really struggling with all the red-tape stuff that delayed everything. But I felt some progress was being made and had to accept these things take time. Boy, did I have sleepless nights though, stomach-churning of epic proportions and of course, my old friend, comfort eating. What's new? I asked myself between stuffing Malteser pills into my chops, yummy, yummy, and a variety of luscious cakes. No mind-numbing pills or the content of a tinny passed my lips, they were a thing of the past. Those dark days when I'd fought to recover from what had happened to me in my second marriage had led me into becoming dependant on some unhealthy props.

As I said earlier, my daughter was very supportive of me finding Shane. She burst into tears one day muttering, "I hate to think of you going through all of this." Being a mum herself, she could comprehend the enormity of losing a child, it was unthinkable for her.

Perhaps it's pertinent to mention here that I haven't delved into lots about my other children because, I wanted to keep focused on this personal story. I will say though that they are grown up with a sense of responsibility and each has two children of their own. I just adore them and love them dearly. In fact, they are wonderful. And I so love being a nan. I'm proud they've turned out well-adjusted adults. That's a great achievement and I pat myself on the back that my screwed-up-ness didn't mess them up. Although I will add that I haven't had contact with my son and his wife, or seen my beautiful grandchildren for some years due to a family dispute. I feel there's a real injustice in this and it has caused me so much pain, yes, the blame's been piled on me again, another dose to deal with. There is always hope though, I live with the fact that all may come well in the future.

Do you know what I find so frustrating in life? It's that people won't take responsibility for the way they treat others. They actually refuse point blank to see how they are acting or have acted, they won't discuss it and don't want to look at it, standing determined they are right no matter what. As a counsellor, I have seen the magical changes that happen when people are open to discussion, looking at their issues, their behaviour and ways of thinking. In learning to have an all-round view of things, and trying to see it from the other person's perspective, I have learnt how healthier relationships are built.

Norcap allocated me a support worker, a lovely lady who I found I could easily talk to. We had had to arrange a meeting to discuss my search and this was duly put in place. It was interesting skulking around a large department store near the café. Several people eyed me up, I remember thinking let them think what they like, they would never guess in a million years why I was there prowling about. I had some details of what she looked like but the more I gave shoppers the once over the more confused I got. However, I suddenly had a feeling about a lady walking towards the café entrance, that's her I thought, I just knew it, and it was. Perhaps we should have carried a copy of the Times, (which I have never read I may add!) or have a flower in our hair, it might have made it more fun and lessened my anxiety. I chose a seat facing a wall, I felt less conspicuous that way. Clutching my coffee, I stared, eyes glistening at this lady, who was no more than a stranger.

"It's nice to meet you in person, Mary, do you feel comfortable where we are sitting?" Her voice held kindly concern.

"I'm alright sitting here, thank you, but I do feel really nervous. I'm not sure what you want to know." A tear trickled down my cheek and I roughly brushed it off my skin.

She pushed a tissue across the table towards me, I took it and dabbed at my face removing some of my makeup in the doing. I started to speak but the words fell away and I slumped back in the chair. The noise around me triggered some irritation and I squirmed around on the hard chair. Does this place know how bloody uncomfortable these chairs are I thought? Don't they have any idea I am here to talk about my lost son, my precious baby? Can't they all just shut up? Do the waitresses really have to clatter the crockery so loudly and scrape the damned chairs on the floor when they push them under the tables? It's all so bloody nerve-jangling. Even the smell of the freshly ground coffee failed to excite my taste buds as it usually did.

*You're being purely irrational in your thinking, Mary,* another voice chuntered in my head.

"Mary, I know this isn't easy but I would like you to explain why you want to find your son?"

My head shot up and I stared at her, what an incredulous question to ask! Why do I want to find my son? Surely, she knew not to ask something so stupid! I found strength and discovered my voice had power as I answered. "Gosh, that seems a really stupid question to ask. I'll tell you why, I'm his mum and I can't stand living without knowing if he is safe, how he is and if life has been kind to him. I need to be able to stop wondering where he is, what he's doing, is he well. It wasn't my choice to have him adopted, I was forced into it by others who felt they knew best, well they didn't! He is my son and I can't go on not knowing anymore?"

My shoulders shook as I gasped for air, it felt like someone had fixed a suction pump onto my chest and was sucking all of it out, I couldn't breathe. I shuddered and felt the tightness in my chest lessening and my breathing became more normal. Phew, a sigh of relief puffed its way out.

She placed her hand over mine which now lay limp on the table, I didn't react but just sat there feeling the warmth of another human being seeping into me. No words were spoken but they weren't necessary, touch was enough to comfort me.

"I hope I didn't sound rude?" was all I managed to say.

"It's all right, I do understand, I liked your passion for finding him." She spoke softly and patted my hand. We went on to talk about how the search would proceed, drank our coffees, exchanged some pleasantries and then she was gone, reassuring me we would talk on the telephone soon.

I had so needed to crawl into a safe, warm bed but I couldn't, so I bought more coffee and a slice of cake and just sat thinking of nothing really, allowing the noise to swirl around me, all irritation had gone.

She rang a few days later to enquire how I was and explained she would be in touch when there was some news. So, the wait began.

# Chapter 18
## *Waiting*

It is unbelievable how time can suddenly cease to have its usual momentum; well, that's how it felt to me. Everything I did took extra effort and I became a great clock watcher, as well as a telephone ringing listener and a letter box clatterer looker-outer. My stress levels rose and flew off the scale and night-times were the worst, thrashing around, tossing and turning until my quilt was either half on the bed, on the floor or wrapped around me so tightly I had to fight my way out.

My ears became big like Dumbo's, it was like they were moving around trying to pick up the sound of the telephone ringing, hone in on anything that might be bringing me news, good news I hoped. Heart-lurching moments occurred when I saw the postman strolling down the drive, I'd been staring at the clock trying to whizz the hands around to make his visit happen quicker. Guess, whose house became the cleanest of the clean? Yes, mine. I was forever busy, vacuuming, dusting, sorting cupboards not once but several times, rushing here, rushing there filling the minutes, hours and days. Manic Mary is my name now.

Finding comfort from my angelic friends, spirit guides and the network of spiritually aware community I had become involved in really helped. However, at the end of the day, it is a lonesome journey.

I won't draw out in minute detail the journey with Norcap. My support lady was very understanding—as she should be—and I could ring or e-mail her when I needed to talk and off-load.

The search went on and on, every day was a challenge for me, and although I was kept up to date with things, sadly there was disappointment after disappointment. But I somehow was managing to claw my way through it all. I amazingly found the strength to keep going and going and going.

Sometimes though, I wailed despondently, T*his is a no-hoper!* Grief seems to have many strands to it: they float and twist around and twine you up in a gargantuan tangle of mixed emotions, agonising thoughts and a rigour-morticed body (without the death thing.) When I was asked by concerned, interested friends if there was any news, I felt like telling them to shut it! I hated saying no, that sounded so final. So, I would say, "Not yet, but I'm sure, there will be soon."

"Never mind, I'm sure they'll trace him," was the standard reply.

But I do mind. Yes of course so very much! And the months rolled endlessly on.

Ring, ring. My elephantine ears flapped. Ring, ring. What oh… Grabbing the phone, a familiar voice spoke, "Hello, Mary, it's…from Norcap."

Hands shaking, belly rumbling, I sat quickly down. "Yes," my trembling voice stumbled a reply.

"Mary, we've traced two of his children via Facebook, they have double-barrelled names, which really complicated the search. Our researcher is also following up with leads to track down their mother. We don't know if this will eventually lead us to Shane, hopefully, it will for your sake. Isn't it amazing after all these months there is some good news. I'm really happy for you."

It felt as if there were hundreds of layers in my brain for this information to filter through, it didn't feel real, it was so hard to comprehend. I just couldn't take it in and I couldn't utter a single word either. I think this lovely lady sensed my struggle at my lack of words.

"Ring me tomorrow Mary, and we'll talk some more when you've taken this all in, I can go into detail about some of what we've learnt, sadly we aren't able to pass on everything I'm afraid. Don't worry, love, we are making some progress now."

"Ok," and I put the phone down in a stupor.

Nearly a year had passed since this vigorous search began; you begin to think nothing will ever be discovered. I realised you can never really be prepared for this sort of phone call when it comes, I certainly wasn't!

I did ring Norcap hoping, fingers crossed there would be more news, but in the end, I just had to accept that some information was confidential. Looking back, I guess people they'd talked to didn't want me contacting them personally, that's quite understandable. There was a protocol to be followed apparently with this organisation. Huh cut the crap I remember thinking, just sort it, get on with it, don't prolong the agony!

Please, please God, whoever or whatever is out there let him be found. Time crept on, there were lots of twists and turns, people not wanting to give information, changing their minds and changing them back again. It was so difficult to deal with. I prayed, begged, bartered with God. Do miracles happen? They certainly do. Eventually, through various sources, my son was found! Yes, he really was found!

When I was given this information, my support worker told me she had spoken to him, I'd felt like bursting, as though the dress I was wearing was suddenly too small and the seams had started to split open. It seemed like millions of questions wanted to rush out, what did he sound like? Was he pleased I'd searched for him? Did he want to meet me? These were just a few of them.

Some huge force inside me leapt out releasing a massive weight I'd been carrying, lugging around all this time. I felt freer and lighter, as though I'd grown wings and could fly. Of course, I couldn't, but it did feel like that. My heart sang some celestial song. I don't know what the words were, but they were there and it was beautiful. My baby son had been found. But he's not a baby now I had to remind myself. A forlorn part of me cried out, 'I so want my baby back', but he was no more. That is the fact, he is a grown man now and a stranger. However, a small part of me still longed for the baby.

His message to me was this, he wanted to meet me one hundred per cent. "What, oh really, gosh, really, does he, you're sure?" My tremulous voice was filled with sighs. My support worker sounded so happy as she relayed this news. "He really does, Mary," came a clear, calm answer. "He is so sure of what he wants. And that is to meet you!"

He wants to meet me, meet me, meet me, on and on it echoed in my head. I had wanted to dance and sing. Meet me. I was laughing, crying, excited, nervous, shaking, there were so many emotions. Feelings and thoughts cascaded through me, I felt I was going to explode, everything was a jumble. I couldn't grasp onto one thing; it was all a shambles.

Another call from my support worker came, explaining that when she had spoken to Shane again (here I am going to keep calling him by the name given to him by his adoptive parents, which is David) and during the call, it was obvious he had been drinking; he was slurring his words and also swore a lot. I was shocked, the image I had of this person and their life, just didn't fit. You see, I was sure he had gone to a posh family and had lived in an upmarket area of London. I was still hanging onto illusions and must face the truth. His adoptive parents were not posh nor did they live in a posh area; in fact, it was a rough area. Please don't think I am condoning his parents, or being a snob, not at all, this was what my mind had created. I wanted the best for him, and I am sure it helped me feel better, less guilty. In my young mind, London had been the capital of wealth. How wrong I was!

For some reason after this latest phone conversation, the hand of dread seemed to take hold, I wondered whether this was going to pan out all right or be a disaster. 'All right' versus 'disaster' batted back and forth in my head; my exuberance had been replaced by such a low. I felt I was being dragged back into the past when so many things didn't work out, it seemed to have been a repetitive occurrence in my life, things just don't work out for the best. It's just a mind game really because lots of amazing, wonderful things have happened in my life, it's easy to get caught up in negative thinking though. Pulling myself up short, I rationalised that David had been so shocked at hearing about his birth mother that he had celebrated, been out on the town with his mates. Yes, that was it, nothing more than that.

# Chapter 19
## *A Thread Between Strangers*

At last, I'd climbed to the top of a high mountain and planted my flag of victory on the top. I'd kept pushing through obstacles, retracing footsteps, been led along blind-alleys, but I just soldiered on—I had to find him! This infamous explorer had been intent on discovering that gem, that presumed extinct species, the lost tribe, the buried treasure, looking here and there and at last, the treasure had been discovered.

There I'd been, waiting none too patiently for the meeting of a lifetime. Yes, I would really be with him. It was unbelievable! So many years had gone by, so much pain had been endured, but now we were being brought back together, Mother and Son. It was truly a miracle.

The first time I spoke to David on the telephone felt weird, unreal. Two strangers trying to find a thread of connection between them. This thread was as fine as a gossamer strand from an intricate woven spider's web. I was fearful it would break and drift apart. On the other hand, it could become a new weaving of wonder, just like a web spun in a hedge that is covered in hoar frost, so beautiful. We needed to gently nurture that fragile connecting thread, perhaps we would be able to spin our own web of truth and openness, love and understanding.

* * * *

The town hall clock clicked on eleven o'clock then on past the hour to five past, ten past, fifteen minutes past. I was like a coiled spring, scared that any minute I would spiral out of control and do something really embarrassing; like run up the road screaming: He's not coming! I knew it! Raced through my head. That's typical of my life and my inner doubter of all doubters, garbled on and on hysterically. People would stand and stare until the sound of the blue-lighted wagon brought rescuers and I was carted off to the 'Funny Farm'. I felt trapped between sane and insane, in a no-man's land.

Tears pricked my eyes, I trembled and waves of fear rolled through me like coal dust, black and clingy, gripping onto the hairs in my nostrils and blocking the life force of breath from me, I gasped for fear of dropping dead in the street.

All of a sudden, I'd looked up and stared ahead, my eyes fixated on a throng of people going about their own business. There he was, walking towards me, an image of his dad, although slightly stockier. I began to tremble and my eyes felt as if they were out on stalks trying to reach him before my body did.

My son, oh, my son. I moved robotically, legs stiff, feet heavy.

Then I was flying, like thistledown blown on a gentle breeze. Closer, closer and then close enough to reach out and touch, feel the flesh of my son, my own flesh and blood. This is all so crazy I'd thought. "Oh, David," came out on a whispered breath and I hugged him and there was an explosion of love bursting forth like a shooting star. My love, my baby, my son and I'd stared into those transparent blue eyes, the eyes of his father.

I don't think any mother could describe in words the feelings and emotions that resonated through me, it was such a personal experience. But every time I watched the programme Long Lost Families, I lived the whole experience time and time again with all those mothers in their reunions. I've journeyed with them every step of the way. It certainly helped me heal in a strange kind of way, cathartically freeing me from so many suppressed emotions. It helped support me in moving on.

My son, sadly to say wasn't a well person, Life had led him down many avenues of unhealthy addictions and although he'd done well in his recovery, he struggled at times coping with his bipolar disorder. My fully open, loving heart had constricted at hearing all of this. Amazingly, I'd felt no guilt, I'd been forced into giving him up after all. They who thought they knew best would never know what their authoritative behaviour had led to, how I wish they were able to witness the result of "We know best!"

Thousands of us have suffered the heart-breaking agony of experiencing and enduring the wretchedness of separation from our babies. The stigma of being an unmarried mother and the shame heaped upon us by society gnawed at us through life. A film called *Philomena* is a powerful testimonial to this very thing. I could tell though, that the leading lady had never been through an experience such as this, you cannot act this out, you have to have lived it. I'm sorry, but that's how I feel.

When David and I were settled in the park sipping drinks in the sunshine, a gentle blue sky overhead, the smell of spring flowers wafting around us, the calls of the seagulls colliding together until they became one cacophony of sound, David spoke.

The first thing he asked me was about my older children. I was so shocked as to how such a notion had got into his head.

My words tripped out, "What?" and I just gawked at him in astonishment. "How could I have had older children, I was just fifteen when I became pregnant, you were my first-born."

His eyes misted over and a single droplet of clear liquid trailed out from one eye. I stared at it unable to comprehend where this thinking had come from, this was a weird conversation to be having.

He shifted in his chair, the laughter and babble of the people in the park around us fading away. I couldn't work out from the expression on his face what he might be thinking, then he spoke again.

"My mother, Barbara as you know her told me that you had other children, and that when I was born you didn't want me."

A rage welled up in me, an agonising scream lodged in my throat. I wanted to shake this woman who had lied, who instilled such an unkind damaging idea into his little head. Damn you! What a stupid stupid thing to do. That wasn't the action of a loving mother, but a selfish, fearful one. Look what you've done to my son, Barbara! You've caused him tremendous heartache and instilled a terrible idea into him that wasn't true. How could you be so selfish? He's had to live with this lie all these years; feeling unwanted, feeling rejected by his mother that had given him life, but wanting her other children. Lies, all lies. How cruel of you, Barbara!

Thankfully, the truth was out and amazingly, when she was dying of cancer, she had given him all the letters I had written to her all those years ago. Sadly, he went on to tell me that he had only read a few, they upset him too much and he'd never been given the cassette recording I'd sent either. That recording had been so full of a mother's love, kindness, warmth and compassion. I'm sure it would have helped him, but obviously, she didn't want him to hear my kind words. As I took this in a great sadness welled up inside me. I'd looked at him and with trembling lips managed to speak.

"David, that's so horrible, I just can't take this in, that wasn't true at all." I'd sat immobilised, staring out into the park that had now drained of any colour, everything seemed dull and lifeless. *What else was I going to hear?* trundled through my mind, I braced myself for more shocks. I stared at my son but could read nothing from his expression and went on to say.

"Oh, David, I am so saddened Barbara told you such a terrible thing. If you had read all the letters, you would have known from the content what you'd been told was a lie. It was clear from what I'd written that I loved you. If only your mum had shared them with you all those years ago, you would have been spared all this agony. I'm just astounded and can't think of what more to say right now."

I'd held a fantasy about our meeting, this wonderful reunion like the ones on Long Lost Families that happened.

The happiness, the tears and the happy-ever-after. Why didn't that happen to me? Why couldn't it have been amazing? Why couldn't it have worked out the way I wanted it to? Why? Why? My head began to spin. You know I hadn't thought the pain of all this could get any worse, but it did in that moment hearing what Barbara had told him. It had felt as though something was squeezing my heart and I clutched my chest to try and lessen the pain.

Letters, letters! Something had tried to trickle its way from my mind. I'd scratched my head hoping it would help it along. Yes, of course, didn't Barbara say in one of her letters that my mum had told her I didn't want him? When I had written and explained that wasn't true, she told me in her next letter that she was very upset by this, that she wouldn't have adopted him if she had known this very thing. Did my own mother plant the seed in her mind and fabricate the truth to suit herself? The fact is lies were told and now I was having to deal with the crap that came with this. She's no longer alive so I can't question her about what actually was said, but yet again would my mother tell me the truth? Sadly, I think not.

David looked at me, our eyes locked together, and in that moment, we came to realise that the power of the truth that had been spoken was very healing for him, but so sad for me. I let tears fall and the sun now shining bright, dried them in their tracks, but I didn't care.

"There's something I would like to ask about too, David. There was something in one of your mum's letters that was disappointing, upsetting along with lots of other emotions it invoked. She wrote that you were sitting by her as she wrote this letter to me and that she asked you if you would like to be in contact with me. Apparently, you told her that no you didn't, that your life was alright as it was." I looked at him questionably as I went on to ask, "Is that true, did you really say that?"

He looked at me crestfallen, his eyes became dull. "Mum, that never happened. She never asked me any such thing. I am so sorry that she should tell you that, it must have been very hurtful for you to hear what she said."

"It was hurtful but I am so glad that it didn't happen, but sad that Barbara should tell more lies. I'm feeling angry now so I won't say anything more."

I seemed to drift off as though I was taking myself to some other place to avoid thinking about what I had just heard. We sat in silence until suddenly I became aware, he was speaking to me.

"Mum." I looked up startled, he had called me mum, wow. "Mum, I hope you are happy with me calling you mum. I decided when we first started chatting on the phone that's what I wanted to do." He sat waiting expectantly for an answer.

I cleared my throat, looked at my son and told him with a joyful sound in my voice, "I'm really happy to hear those words, Son, I've dreamt of this day for so long. Maybe it's time for another hot drink, eh?"

As we sat sipping our drinks, more of my son's life emerged. Not a happy story either I'm afraid, listening wasn't easy and I'd felt so helpless. Why, oh, why did it turn out this way? It was all such a mess. It was nice hearing about his son and daughter, but tragically he had lost a baby son, which Barbara had already told me about. I also learnt there was another granddaughter too. My family was growing minute by minute.

It was lovely to hold each other and feel the connection. There still was a part of me that wanted the baby, perhaps that will never totally go away. We moved from the café to sit under a weeping willow tree overlooking the river. This helped ease our overcharged emotions; water is a great healer. We'd decided to meet in Bath which is a beautiful city and happened to be halfway between where we both lived. The colour had started coming back into our world as we sat companionably allowing the magic of our reunion to emerge again.

When it was time to leave, we arranged to meet again the next day, oh how I longed for that next meeting to arrive really quickly.

# Chapter 20
## *Mixed Blessings*

Can you believe it was a warm sunny day again? The pigeons with their deformed feet pecked hungrily around seeking any crumb they could find as we sat by the river. Ducks swam lazily along, quacking at nothing in particular, and the sound of the water rushing over the weir swirled around us. This beautiful backdrop created a peaceful haven. We were wrapped up in ourselves talking about this and that, catching up on all the lost years. But they were just words. All that had been, could never be brought back as an experience, so much had been lost, so much time wasted. It was in reality bittersweet, but one has to accept that is the way it was.

When David related a particular experience to me, I felt my body tense and my hands tremble. My heart pounded loudly at what I was being told. Was I hearing, right? Did his grandfather really treat him so unkindly, make him sit on a stool; rigid with fear while he was shouted at and verbally abused? I shivered at hearing such a vivid replay of the treatment that he had suffered from this person. Apparently, when David had told his mum she wouldn't believe him and that had had a profound effect on his mental state.

Can you believe that one 'special kiss' all those years back had led to so much pain. Perhaps it would have been good if his birth father had been here to witness all of this, what an escape he's had! Later I came to understand that it wasn't full sex either and I hadn't known it was called sex anyway. Just my luck!

My daughter and beautiful grandchildren were so interested in our meeting and rang me to enquire how it went. Bless them. It was such a joy to share how happy I'd felt about seeing him after all these years, I didn't divulge the unsettling things I'd been told, they're for a quiet moment when I see my daughter. The friend I had stayed with too had been really supportive, it all helped, there had been so much to take in, absorb, make sense of.

I'd had to ring my support worker when I got home. However, I decided to leave it a few days to try and make sense of all that had been said and discussed. My brain was on overload for sure, as well as all the overwhelming emotions. I didn't think I could cry much more, but I did.

I told my support worker I felt I had to grieve for the loss of the fantasy I had created around meeting my son and hearing about his wonderful life; that illusion had been shattered. Perhaps I had created this illusion to reassure myself that having him adopted was for the best and that he would flourish in an amazing family and be tremendously happy. How wrong I was!

She was very supportive until she asked me about the physical contact, I had had with him at our meeting. "Well, we had some hugs and a few cuddles in the park, it was nice to have that contact, it had been a long time after all," I answered.

I couldn't believe what she'd said next.

"You have to be careful, Mary, that this physical contact doesn't lead to a sexual relationship, as so often can happen in these cases."

Christ, what is she going on about? I'd felt sick, and trembling grabbed a chair and plonked myself down on it. I remember clearly the reply I had come back with. "What the hell are you insinuating?" I quizzed angrily. "A sexual relationship, bloody hell what a thing to say. I don't fancy my son, I love him, I'm his mother after all."

She answered in a calm manner. "Well, these reunions often lead to this sort of thing happening, and as your support worker, I am obliged to check this out with you as it's part of our policy. I'm sorry I have upset you and obviously what I said has shocked you."

"You can say that again," I growled. "Such a thing had never entered my head; I feel all of what you're saying has tainted something that was just a natural warmth between two people brought back together after years of being apart. Can't I even enjoy being with him without such a horrible thing being planted into the equation?"

I ended our conversation and decided I didn't want any more contact. Perhaps I was being irrational but I didn't want more of this sex stuff. After all, that's what caused this whole situation in the first place, that bloody 'special kiss' has a lot to answer for. And I so wish that dratted lone sperm hadn't made it to its destination.

\* \* \* \*

Train journeys to London meant we could meet some more and I got to see my grandson too. David wasn't in touch with either of his daughters at that stage. I'd learnt that he'd had another daughter with his first wife. However, it all felt a little strange, there seemed to be something missing, but I couldn't quite put my finger on it. I enjoyed exchanging texts from time to time but we didn't speak every day. Sometimes I knew he had been drinking, but he always apologised, especially if he swore. At these times, my heart sank.

I began to feel that things weren't going so well, I felt I couldn't give him what he wanted and I didn't know what that was either. Falling into the 'why don't things work out for me' and 'why can't they just be easy for once' brought on a bout of depression, but not so intense as I had suffered in the past.

We discovered we both ate with the fork in our right hand and believe it or not, David had had some psychic experiences, it felt unwise to mention the thing-a-ma-bob things that had happened to me though. And I'm not going to enlarge on this here either, all I will say is it was really scary.

In my cupboard is a jumper he bought me from Camden Lock Market, it's so treasured. He didn't have lots of money and although I bought him small things or a meal or two, I didn't feel it wise to lavish him with lots of stuff or give him cash. I felt we needed to build on our relationship before I became more generous. Perhaps hearing him mention several times along the way about having to meet his rental payments, getting phone top-ups, etc. made me wary. Yet I was aware he was managing to buy alcohol and at times, cannabis. Also, I had a sense of loyalty to my other children, isn't it about fairness? Who knows? My prime focus was to get to know each other and work out how I could support him. If I had lavished him with money and gifts, I would have felt I was buying him. And these thoughts had so stirred up memories of tying up the paper work for his adoption with the solicitor: money was a sensitive issue.

I remember so well the evening he rang when I was in a restaurant waiting for friends, it was my birthday and near to Christmas, a festive time I love. We chatted for about ten minutes and then as my guests arrived, I enquired whether I could ring him later, I knew he didn't go to bed early.

"That's fine, we'll speak later he replied." He seemed quite happy and we finished our call after a few more pleasantries, I told him I so looked forward to continuing our chat when I got home. There was no indication of what was to come.

Thirty minutes later, a text came through and it read: **'What's more important, your friends, food, drink or me? I never heard from my son again.'**

Through texts, I tried my best to encourage him to speak with me, but unfortunately, I never had a response of any sort. He'd never given me his address in London so I couldn't write, and although I contacted Norcap to explain what had happened they were unable to intervene. I've had to grieve my son a second time and the soreness in my heart was like having had a dagger stuck in it. Life is so cruel!

You may be asking yourselves how I coped with the unfortunate outcome of being reunited with my adopted son. I certainly was a miserable person for some time and the old feelings of being a victim were very powerful. Why me? This doesn't happen to anyone else; I might have known it wouldn't work out, etc. became an irritant inside my head. Anger, grief and pain would collide with each other at times and then all would become calm. I came to realise his feelings of insecurity and abandonment were triggered and it was too much for him to cope with. What was very interesting were the feelings of committing suicide which I'd had in the past when things got tough didn't happen. That was a surprise! I had lots of support from friends and family, but when you live on your own and you wake in the dead of night and it all crowds in, it is a mighty lonely place to be.

# Chapter 21
## *An Unexpected Happening*

When I had been thinking all was lost and was wallowing in my misery and had embarked on writing this story, a miracle happened. I had a message via Facebook from David's ex-wife asking if I wanted to be in touch with my grandchildren. Oh, the joy, the happiness I felt my spirits lift and felt hopeful.

At first, I was a little hesitant; was I going to open myself up to more disappointment and sadness and end up worse off? Was it better to leave things as they were, let the past stay in the past, get on with my life accepting David couldn't handle any ups and downs in our relationship? I had come to an understanding that as soon as I couldn't speak when he wanted, he felt rejected and abandoned again. Was my need to have a relationship with my son a selfish want? In reality, I think it is a natural response to wanting to have my son in my life.

Strangely while writing this; it's now 2020, a revelation filtered through many levels of my mind which made me aware of something very important, something that I had realised years ago but pushed to the back of my mind. But here it was yet again. All these years, I had yearned, longed for my baby, the little one I was denied keeping and looking after, stopped from sharing all those precious moments that come with having children. I had only one thing in my mind and that was, "I wanted my baby back!" Oh, how strong that has been since he was taken from me. I've kidded myself at times, focusing on the grown man, but there deep within me lay the yearning for my baby still. The thousands of tears I've shed; the misery I've experienced along life's way by the haunting of this experience have been difficult to deal with. Though there has been joy, laughter and immense love being a mum to my other two children that came some years later. Everything had become such a tangled mass in my mind.

However, over the years, I've sorted out this mass strand by strand; obviously, there could still be more to unravel and make sense of. The workings of the mind are a very complex thing. This is a revelation that pushed its way into my mind one day. If I continue to hold onto his baby self, keep him with me, then David has this part of him missing. He isn't whole because I have held onto his baby self mindfully, emotionally and energetically.

Now being a therapist of long standing, I could understand this but had never been aware of the consequences of what my heartbreak of losing him in the flesh and never being able to grieve had created.

Strangely, I was having counselling—yet again—and could talk this through. The counsellor was so kind and supportive. A plan was made as to how I could let my baby go to where he should rightfully be; with David.

Amazingly, as I write having worked at and followed through with different processes, I feel freer, I don't long for my baby like I used to anymore, and that is wonderful. What

I feel for my baby now is totally selfless and has led me to a love for David I was never aware of.

But there is a shadow lurking, that haunts me inside at times still. A shadow of that baby that is clinging on and I'm party to that clinging too. But this shadow is not a tangible thing and in time that too dissolved away.

# Chapter 22
## *New Connections*

Well, I was now messaging my new grandchildren through Facebook. Isn't this technology wonderful? It has brought so many people together and I am so grateful for that. Getting to know these two children was a bit nerve-racking but exciting too. Receiving messages from them was a joy and being rather eager to learn all about them I had to restrain myself from bombarding them with lots of questions.

But gradually, over time, we found our way and I felt a natural connection between us, that was a real blessing. One of the saddest things I learnt was that their dad was not in contact with either of them now. I so hoped that maybe, just maybe there would be a miracle and somehow David and I would reconnect again and all would be well between us all. I've been a real fix-it person in my life and have found it frustrating when I haven't been able to render something fixed.

I decided early on that it was right to talk to my daughter and grandchildren about having two new grandchildren in my life, after all, they are so important to me and dearly loved. They were so understanding and of course interested to learn more about them, and many enjoyable conversations followed between us.

I must admit it did feel a little strange to suddenly have some more family in my life, but something that triggered spine-tingling and heart-fluttering moments when I thought of them. Although I had met Joe when I saw his dad in London years ago, I had never met Hope. But it was going to happen, really happen; we were to meet up!

A plan was put together. I was going to travel up to Paddington by train and we would meet in the station. I think it would have helped if we'd been specific about where that would be. But of course, we had mobile phones, which I will say played a useful part in us getting together.

I was so happy and had this dream that I would be able to bring this family back together again (here I go again trying to fix it!) and all would be a happy-ever-after scenario. Well, that's typical of me to indulge in a fantasy. My childhood happy-ever-after fairy tale endings still played out in my mind. Looking back how many did have happy endings? Not a lot!

\* \* \* \*

In amongst all of this, and the happiness I was feeling, I was to learn that my son had suffered a stroke and had been in hospital. Although now back home, he needed carers to help with so many things having lost movement in some parts of his body. This was a shock to hear and I felt helpless as to how I could help him. Then I went into a dark place: what if he should die before we make our peace? Or have found some way of building a friendship, and what sort of friendship could that be? What if I died? It doesn't bear thinking about!

I managed to contact David's ex-wife and obtain his phone number; but what should I do? It was scary to think of ringing him but worse still not to. I know he didn't like answering his phone unless he knew who it was. What did I have to lose by ringing? It couldn't make it any worse surely? I gave myself a good talking to and decided I had to be brave. Here goes. As the number rang out, I found myself quivering, my heart was thumping loudly. It got to the sixth ring and suddenly a male voice said, "Hello."

Taking a deep breath, I asked, "Is that David?" And held my breath waiting for an answer.

"Yes, but who's asking?" I could sense the uncertainty in his voice.

"David, it's mum, I heard you were unwell and so wanted to know how you were doing."

I was a little taken aback as he went on to chat in a friendly way as if everything was alright.

It was a good conversation and he told me it was good to hear from me and he didn't want it to end the way, it did last time. That brought joy to my heart and I started feeling confident that this would all turn out well. It was as if a bright rainbow had started shining in my life.

# Chapter 23
## *London, Here I Come*

I raced to the train station having misread my clock and gasping for breath leapt on the train, fumbled for my ticket and once I had my bearings made my way to my seat. Flashing my ticket at the stranger who was sitting there as proof 'this seat is mine' the stranger with a grumpy look on his face reluctantly moved.

My mind raced with the 'what ifs?' Was there another train if I'd missed this one? They'd perhaps think I didn't really want to meet them. I'd have to pay again as my ticket wasn't transferable! In the end, I told myself to shut up and ate a now crumpled sandwich which had somehow got squashed banana all over it!

Right, Mary, just enjoy the journey and do your usual thing of spotting Herons, one of my favourite birds. The countryside started to flash by, it looked so dark and dank out there but even in winter, the countryside has an appeal to me. The cows stood with their heads bent, looking bedraggled and sorry for themselves. Torrents of rain started to splatter the windows and gradually they steamed up. Well, that was the end of the heron spotting!

The elderly lady next to me started chatting and between our chats and food munching before I knew it, we were nearly at Paddington. I'd explained to the lady why I was going to London and she became excited and enthused over what a wonderful meeting it was going to be for me. This kindly lady will never know how she lifted my spirits and I felt more positive.

Well, here I am standing on a noisy platform, my eyes darting everywhere as I made my way to the information point. Hope had texted to say where she would be, but when I got there crowds of people milled around and I couldn't make out who were couples, singles or folk just loitering for no reason. I did have a vague idea of what she looked like from her Facebook image but didn't know she'd had her hair cut. Three circuits and I bravely walked up to a young lady who was furiously dabbing at her mobile: how do these youngsters text so fast?

"Hello," I nervously asked, "are you Hope by any chance?"

She looked at me and smiled, a warm smile at that and responded happily. "Nan," and gave me a lovely hug.

We started chatting and immediately felt comfortable in each other's company. Apparently, Joe was nowhere to be seen so she was frantically ringing to find out where he was. At last, we found him, standing on the slip road into the station amongst crowds of people rushing backwards and forwards.

Joe was so pleased to see me and we hugged spontaneously. I was so happy, my new family with me we wandered off to a local restaurant for lunch—my treat of course. As it was near Christmas, I had brought them a gift as a surprise, I'd so enjoyed choosing them and packing them in colourful paper.

Do you know? I could not believe how well we got on and settled at our table which was in the perfect spot for private conversation. I told them I was happy to answer any questions they had and openly did so. I could tell my answers were helping them to understand more about their dad and that certain things Barbara (his mum) had told him had really affected his well-being, as had his grandfather's unkind treatment of him. At times I've felt frustration at the way Barbara had handled things. However, I understand that her fear of losing David was so great that it had led her to saying these things, that's so sad. I've often pondered how would I have dealt with all this? But my compassionate heart feels nothing but kindness and forgiveness for her now.

Joe wondered why one of his names was 'Shane' and I was able to explain I'd named his dad Shane Richard when he was born.

A joy for me was to tell them that I had been talking to their dad and that he had told me he would love to be in contact with them again. I told them I had encouraged him with that and that hopefully building my own relationship with him would help him to find a way of doing so, with them. Here I go again trying to make it all better. I'd spent so much time and effort trying to sort out my parents as a child. It's become a real habit with other situations and not a healthy one at that! But I know better now and pulled myself up short. I couldn't believe what I heard myself saying next when I related the story of a colleague at work; who in a matter-of-fact way, had just blurted out: 'You're obviously going to have a baby.' I was a very immature fifteen-year-old then.

Confusion followed as to how that might have happened. "Well, I thought when something strange happened one

146

evening that hadn't occurred before, that it was 'a special kiss'. But I was to learn later it was a thing called 'sex' and that it hadn't even been proper sex."

How I coloured up, flustered by what I'd said. Looking at their faces they didn't seem perturbed at all. I suddenly gave a big sob and a few sly (I'm interested as to why I have written the word 'sly' here, David's father's surname was Sly!) tears escaped my then scrunched up eyes, amazingly they both jumped up and hugged me.

This time was so special, so magical and my heart sang. I explained that I had brought them a little Christmas gift, and no they shouldn't be embarrassed that it was a joy for me to give them a present. After all, it was only a few weeks until the festive season started.

Joe laughed and said, "It's alright as long as it isn't socks, everyone seems to think I need socks. Why don't we open them now while you're here?"

I couldn't believe what I was hearing, I was in such a panic, as guess what? I had bought him socks, bright multi-coloured beautiful ones. I don't know how I had managed not to react; I just told him that it would be nice if they opened them at Christmas and that they needn't feel guilty they hadn't bought me anything. Phew.

This meeting was one of such joy and happiness. We got on so well and were comfortable in each other's company. Oh, I felt so blessed and happily paid the bill. The fact that they really respected me and didn't take advantage of me by ordering lots from the menu meant a lot to me.

When we left, I decided to go to Camden Lock a place that I had visited with David years ago when we'd first met in London. Hope and Joe took me to the right bus stop and we said our farewells. I would have loved to have spent more time with them. Feeling so elated with happiness and joy, I accepted they had other things to do. My decision to go to Camden Lock was a big mistake. It was packed, noisy and I felt a headache come on. I just had to get out of that place; I fled, dashed to a bus stop and made my way back to Paddington.

Strangely, I felt overwhelmed by the whole thing, the wonderful time with my grandchildren and the happy memories of being with my son years before brought tears to my eyes. I still have and treasure the jumper David had bought me from the Campden market when we spent time there.

At last, I could get on my train and a surprise message came through from Hope, a touching message, at that, and I returned one likewise.

Two friendly ladies shared my table seat on the train and I told them my story and they were thrilled for me. I found it very moving to tell my tale. (I didn't mention the special kiss thing though.) When one of these ladies came back from the buffet car, she gave me a small bottle of wine so that I could celebrate when I got home. It was such a kind thoughtful thing to do. How blessed I felt, how happy to have these fellow travellers to chat to.

My wise self prompted me though: *do not expect every meeting to be like this one, this was the extra special super-duper one. Don't have huge expectations of what your next meeting will be like.* Thank you, wise self, for I could easily have fallen into that trap and must take each time we get together as a special time in its own right.

I guess I was on a high for a long time and shared my happiness and joy with friends and family. More texts were exchanged and that was a lovely feeling. However, I knew I mustn't rush things, or put any pressure on them. My over-excitable nature can take over from my sensible self at times.

# Chapter 24
## *David*

I was enjoying the telephone calls I was having with David and sometimes just the simple texts that arrived. His health was beginning to improve although he still had carers going in to help out. He'd amazingly given me his address and it was nice to send him a mobile top-up now and again; at least I felt I was helping him out, it was nice to hear his appreciation too.

During this period of time, I never heard any slurring in his voice and hoped his addictions were now a thing of the past and that he was managing to find some sense of peace in his life; I do hope so!

As human beings, can we ever really know what's going on in someone's mind? The mind to this day is still not 100% fully understood. Although I do think there are some couples, partners who over the years have come to understand somehow what their partners are thinking. Perhaps they are just good at guessing! Or maybe they have a really powerful connection, not just as human beings but on a spiritual level too.

David and I talked about meeting up when he was feeling better and able to get out and about more. I know he had a young man in his life with whom he had a close platonic relationship. I came to learn that this person was a sort of unofficial adopted son. From what I heard he was a great support.

It was decided by David that as I had kindly sent him several mobile top-ups, he would ring me the next time and we arranged a day. Mulling this over, I thought it would be a shame if he rang when I was seeing clients so I texted to say I was so looking forward to his call, but it was best to avoid the time when I was working and gave him the information. It was clear in my mind that I didn't want him to think I was avoiding him; we all have stuff happening throughout our day.

The day dawned for him to ring and a trickle of excitement flowed through me. I felt his offer of contacting me was a sign he respected me. I waited and waited, clock-watching but the minutes slowly ticked by, those minutes became hours, my chest felt tight and I could hardly breathe as dread took over. I checked all my clocks and phone to see if I had the right time and of course, they all showed the correct time. Time dragged on and I kept rethinking what could have gone wrong. I got more and more stressed, upset and depressed, here we go again I thought. And guess what? He never rang and I have never heard from him to this day. I've rung, texted and written but to no avail. There is just an empty space where a friendship could have been growing.

Again, I had lost my son and the pain was still as bad; a soreness settled in my heart and I felt despondent once more. Maybe it would have been better to set a time for his call when we had arranged the day. What more could I have done? If he'd rung and I was with a client, on the loo, in the shower, I have a feeling the same thing would have happened.

Thankfully, I was still in touch with his children, my grandchildren so that is an amazing thing that has come out of all this. I so hope that goes well. I've no fantasies about what will happen, but feel very grounded in my thinking. Of course, I get my insecurities popping up at times but rationalise them to settle myself.

# Chapter 25
## *A Call to Dartmoor*

As time passed, I felt inspired to go to Dartmoor and carry out a loving, spiritual ritual around letting go of my son; all the pain, disappointment and stress I have experienced. But also to pray for his safekeeping, well-being and a new understanding of the choices around the lifestyle he has chosen: there are other healthier ways.

My friend Nell drove us to the moors. The day was bright, calm and peaceful. I had with me a beautiful heart-shaped pink quartz crystal along with flower heads, small and colourful, carefully carried in a polythene bag, having been gently sprayed with cool water.

We took a path that climbed gently along a twisting track. Although my breathing became laboured, I knew this sojourn was going to result in something special happening. As the vista opened up, I felt so peaceful, this was so right. I felt nature was nurturing me leading me to a place of healing.

And then I saw it, a huge boulder formation to my left, not too far off the track; it just sat there. It had a huge smile formed across it from a gap in the rock formation. I was drawn to it; I smiled and felt a warm glow inside me. There appeared to be a pair of eyes, a nose, ears and I felt this amazing energetic connection. I was moved to tears. "This is the place, Nell," I mumbled at her.

"Yes, I feel it's calling too." Nell gently touched my arm. "You know Mary, this tor is **Rippon Tor**. How incredible is that." She smiled kindly.

Just that one smile helped and comforted me. Friends are so special and so important in our lives.

I started to move slowly around this boulder, drawn by its energy field, feeling completely at one with it. As I circled around, I scattered the flower heads with a heartfelt intention of letting my son go, of him somehow finding peace within himself and thanking him for being my son. As the tears fell, I felt a great relief and my heart opened with such tenderness. I was experiencing the strongest love, I had ever felt for him and the more I let go, the more this love flowed from my heart.

I then held the rose quartz heart-shaped crystal in my hand and prayed so hard that we would always be connected by our hearts; that some mystical, magical happening would take place between us. I stretched my hand out into a gap in this large, grey boulder and my fingers touched the edge of an indentation. I gently placed the crystal in what I thought was a dip where it could nestle.

A cry of amazement left me as the crystal fell down through what was actually a hole, to rest forever in this place, known only to myself and my friend. It would never be found unless the boulder blew apart; it could never be tainted, never taken, but would always rest in the peace that I was now feeling. I so wished that my son would feel this too.

Turning to Nell, I muttered, "It's amazing the boulder has become the keeper of the crystal, a hole has enveloped it for safekeeping; it's incredible." It feels so right so...o...o...wonderful, I could sing with joy. Of course, I cried, but not tears of sadness; they were tears of relief in feeling freer and happier. It felt complete.

We hugged and continued up the path to a tor way up, the wind swirled around us; my hair danced wildly, tickling my face. High up, the clouds changed form, shutting the rays of warm sunlight out, then allowing the warmth once more to nurture my body. The ground rose and fell, scattered with rocks, flora and fauna of different hues painting a landscape of nature that was so beautiful, reaching out into the distance until it kissed the horizon.

\* \* \* \*

Life goes on. One adjusts and builds on what is there, not what isn't there. David certainly wasn't a part of my life. Acceptance of a situation frees the mind from its mutterings, it's if-only this, if-only that; the what could have been, or not been. Things can eat away at you. It just wasn't working with David and me, but a part of me will never give up hope. It's there lurking in the back of my mind, waiting to emerge at the minutest opportunity, however fragile that might be. I would never have thought that I would be back at Smiley Rock in the not-too-distant future, or the reason for that visit either.

# Chapter 26
## *Heavy Feet, Heavy Heart*

I've got to get there! I can't waste any time! I was all of a jitter, hands shaking, heart pounding as I raced around gathering warm clothes, waterproofs and a rucksack and shoved numerous eatables into its depths. I was just about to slam the door when I realised I didn't have my car keys or any money; w*hat a fool you are, Mary, slow down*!

I must go, it's the place where I can gain some sense of solace. Well, I damn well hope so! Somehow, the months had slipped by since I'd had the lovely experience at Smiley Rock, it has so calmed me and a photo has been displayed on my mantelpiece ever since. It's a great comfort to me. I've just had to accept that David and I are not going to be as mother and son. Too many years have gone by and too much has happened. In fact, the damage was done a long, long time ago. His pain and feelings of abandonment and rejection ran so deep in him, that there's nothing I can do to change all of that or even some of that.

But now, the worst has happened. I gathered some sort of composure so I could drive safely. The miles slipped by, the noise of the rain at times slashed against the car, the windscreen wipers did their best. Gradually, the inside windows steamed up, my erratic fumblings with the heater controls had messed up the temperature, creating blurred vision. All that kept running through my mind was the song 'Steamy Windows' by? Oh, I don't know, does it really matter who sang the darn song anyway? So, I stopped in a layby and cleaned the windows, so I could see clearly again.

A car roared by, right through a deepish collection of water right alongside me, just as I'd started to open the driver's door. I screamed, shouted and swore as I was soaked by a sudden rush of water spraying over me from this lunatic in charge of the vehicle. I started stamping and swearing some more. The air turned blue, so to speak, and huffing and puffing, I slumped into my seat and cried. Once my tirade was finished, I started the engine and drove on, at least the rain was easing now. I began chanting, "I'm safe, secure and protected," to keep my mind focused. But then gave up in despair.

At last, I arrived at my destination, or so I thought! Where is it, where's the car park, where's the damn tor? Right, I'm parking here and that's it! And as I slammed the car door shut, turned and looked up through the mistiness of the rain, it came into view. Rippon Tor, and up there, near the brow was Smiley Rock. I'm wet and cold, but I don't care, I just need to climb up, to be there, to find some form of comfort to ease my aching heart.

The words kept slamming around in my head, those words I never expected to read, but I did read them, and they somehow filled my body, like large rocks, making it almost impossible to move. I felt so weighted down.

As I trudged up the tor, each footstep an effort to take, the words became louder in my head, much louder. I've got to let them out, they're going to explode my brain with the power and pressure I'm feeling inside my skull.

What was it my grandson had written through my Facebook messenger? "Hello, Nan, I'm sorry I haven't been in touch, have been going through a lot. I'm sorry to have to inform you that my dad your son has died." I couldn't read anymore.

That's why I'm here, running from the sight of that message, running from that dreadful word 'died'. But it was here with me, inside my skull filling me with horror. Dead? No, David my son; Shane, the baby I gave birth to. All that I endured over the years and he's dead. No no no! Not dead?

There's no hope now, that's all been swiped away in one word 'died'. The fantasy of how I wanted it to be, dreamt of it, prayed for a happy ending; now gone. It's impossible to have because he's dead!

Heavy-footed and heavy-hearted, I clambered on. Slipping over rocks, sliding on the mud, getting wetter and wetter, but it didn't matter, nothing mattered now.

At last, I was there! Gasping for breath after such a steep climb, chilled to the bone but there nonetheless. I grappled in the bottom of my rucksack and my fingers clasped the pink quartz crystal I'd grabbed on the way out. David, your crystal is already here inside this boulder and now mine will be too; we will always be connected through our hearts, not in the way I wanted, but for me, this is as special as it can get. Fumbling fingers clutched the crystal as I traced them along the long gap in the rock, (although it's more of a huge boulder really!) Suddenly the crystal dropped from my frozen fingers down to join the other crystal. My heart opened and love poured out, and then the sobs broke from deep within and I sat in the drizzle on a nearby rock and cried the deepest pain I'd ever felt, it went on and on but it didn't matter. This emotional outburst continued until I was exhausted. I just sat staring into space, until I looked up at the clouds, heavy and grey, scudding across the expanse that rose over the moor. Everything seemed bleak, all around me, above me and inside of me.

I eventually made my way back to my car, being careful not to fall. I drove home in a state of bewilderment but aware the two rose quartz crystals were a symbol of our connection. That helped somewhat. And Smiley Rock would forever be there protecting these precious crystals and all they signified.

* * * *

It's been an arduous time not being able to see my son's body and say goodbye, and there was no funeral; the pandemic interfered with all of this. However, there was a scattering of his ashes eventually when restrictions were lifted somewhat. That was special being with my grandchildren and sharing such an experience.

I hold onto the fact I have two lovely grandchildren now and can build a future with them. David at least has given me this. I'm blessed with other grandchildren too; they are so precious to me.

Time is a motion we cannot stop, it carries us along, over bumpy roads and smooth ones too.

# Smiley Rock

**DAVID MILANTA (SHANE MEEK) 30.7.64-7.1.2021**

RIP MY SON. YOU'LL NEVER BE FORGOTTEN

*We are but the ripples of life, changing, growing, flowing. There is constant movement, and the cycle of death and rebirth is continuous. Here in this moment, I am a ripple of my mother, my children a ripple of me and their children a ripple of them. An unending continuation through time, and so the generations flow on.*

# A MESSAGE FOR MY READERS

I have felt compelled to write this very personal story as I feel it should be known what agony and emotional turmoil teenagers and women went through, not just at the time, but for most; a continuum through their life, of being separated from their babies, yes, their beautiful babies. For so many, not by a conscious choice of their choosing, but because of the shame and guilt foisted upon them, and the coercion that occurred. Hear enough times that you're too young, not capable, it's for the best, you've no means of supporting yourself, your baby needs a good home, etc: and the undermining sinks deep into oneself until you believe it all. I know, I've had to live with all this and so many regrets.

I so hope that my very personal journey through this book will in some way help others and enlighten those who weren't in this situation.

As my story emerged, I became that vulnerable fifteen-sixteen year old self, gradually making more sense of things as doors that had been closed inside me began to open and she was able, with loving care to heal.

My heartfelt wishes reach out to you all, may you be blessed by Angels as you journey through life, may it be filled with wonderful happenings and most of all that you find peace. You're amazing!

With blessings and love, Mary.

# HISTORIC INFORMATION REGARDING MOTHER AND BABY HOMES

The first of many dedicated 'Mother and Baby Homes' were opened by the Salvation Army in 1890 in Hackney between 1945 and 1980. 20 of these homes were operational across the UK with the last, based in East London, closing in 1980. (Taken from various sources on the internet).

In general, it is reported that an estimated 185,000 women, most of them unmarried teenagers at the time, were coerced into having their babies adopted between 1949 and 1976 in the UK. Many were sent to 'Mother and Baby' homes run by the state, religious or charitable bodies where they were made to feel shame and guilt: some were required to do menial labour. There were a total of 172 known homes for unmarried mothers, the majority run by religious bodies. (Taken from various sources on the internet).

A period in the United States history called the 'Baby Scoop Era' started after the end of World War II and ended in approximately 1972, characterised by an increased rate of premarital pregnancies over the preceding period, along with a higher rate of newborn adoptions. From approximately 1940 to 1970, it is estimated that up to 4 million mothers in the United States surrendered new born babies to adoption, 2 million during the 1960s alone. (Taken from various sources on the internet).

There are many other countries that were involved in these adoption processes too.